deux

Uncover Your Story to Live an
Intuitively Purposeful Life

Dawn Lynn

Spirit Mark
PRESS

Copyright © 2019 Dawn Lynn
All rights reserved.

Printed in the United States of America

Published by Spirit Mark Press, LLC
4498 Main Street, Suite 4 #140
Buffalo, NY 14226-3826

All rights reserved. No part of this publication may be reproduced or transmitted in any form without prior written permission of the publisher.

All examples are based on real individuals. To protect the privacy of these individuals, names and identifying details have been changed.

ISBN-13: 978-0-9990411-3-0
ISBN-10: 0-9990411-3-4

Library of Congress Control Number: 2019931085

*For my mom and dad,
Everything I am is because you planted a seed and
lovingly tended to its needs.*

TABLE OF CONTENTS

Acknowledgements — pg iii

Prologue — pg 1

Section One: Know Your Story

Chapter One:	Energy Expanded	pg 7
Chapter Two:	Genetics	pg 15
Chapter Three:	Parents & Caregivers	pg 27
Chapter Four:	Childhood Peers & Siblings	pg 44
Chapter Five:	Adult Peers	pg 62
Chapter Six:	Institutions	pg 79
Chapter Seven:	School	pg 82
Chapter Eight:	The Workplace	pg 92
Chapter Nine:	Religion	pg 99
Chapter Ten:	The Community	pg 107
Chapter Eleven:	Choice	pg 114
Chapter Twelve:	Tragedy	pg 120
Chapter Thirteen:	Death	pg 132
Chapter Fourteen:	The Experiences	pg 141

Section Two: Manifest Your Dreams

Chapter Fifteen:	Your Story	pg 153
Chapter Sixteen:	What Deux You Want?	pg 157
Chapter Seventeen:	Visualize Your Desires	pg 163
Chapter Eighteen:	Believe It's Possible	pg 177
Chapter Nineteen:	Deux It	pg 186
Chapter Twenty:	Live Purposefully	pg 194
Chapter Twenty-One:	Intuition	pg 209
Chapter Twenty-Two:	Go Forth & Conquer	pg 214

Appendix — pg 217

ACKNOWLEDGEMENTS

Many individuals have made this book possible, and I am blessed that the universe continues to put the right people in my path at the right time.

Jen Holliday, Sue Drozd-Kowalski, Ginny Sukmanowski and Nancy Eckerson, as content editors your unique perspectives are cherished, and the suggestions offered were priceless. More importantly, thank you for being in my life.

Carole Knuth, thank you for not only being a copy editor extraordinaire but also a cheerleader and more importantly, a friend.

Joe Babcock, you are truly a gifted artist and guided by intuition. You were able to decipher my ramblings and bring the concept of Deux to life with the logo. Thank you!

Don. Where do I begin? You sacrificed to make this book possible – the long days as Mr Mom, the nights apart with me holed up in a hotel for some quiet and the weeks away. Thank you for supporting me in all my endeavors.

Last but not least, each of you who read *One*, who loved it and asked for more. I was humbled by the reception of the first book and volume of individuals who not only requested, but in some instances hounded me for the next book. Well, my friends, here it is. I hope you love it because without you, I'd be an author without a cause.

PROLOGUE

During the writing of *One: Unleashing the Energy that Connects Us All*, I knew there would be books "Two" and "Three" as there were concepts that deserved exploration but were outside of the primary objective of *One*. Those concepts and content were placed in a parking lot with the intention of flushing out *Two* and *Three* in the future. When I sat down to write *Two*, I, naively and perhaps somewhat pompously, believed sitting down to pen this book would be easy. It wasn't.

The reasons writing this book were more challenging should have been anticipated. For example, while writing *One*, my daughter was a toddler who was easily preoccupied and corralled. Now she is an active and strong-willed preschooler, and the strategies my husband and I utilized to give me time to write the first book were not as successful for the writing of *Two*. In fact, half of this book was written with my daughter sitting squarely on my lap typing on her iPad as I typed on my computer. Additionally, just as with *One*, where the premise and the objective of the book changed while being fleshed out, I had the same experience with *Two*. To my dismay and excitement, it became clear early in the process that what I had in mind was not what the universe intended. As a result, every time I sat down to write, rather than words flowing seamlessly, the only sound that cut through the silence was that of my own heartbeat.

Then one day, when I let go of my time frame and my expectations, inspiration struck.

While much of the book evolved, the core purpose didn't. This book, as was originally intended, is a follow-up to *One* and the belief that we are connected as one universal energy that facilitates intuition. *One* explored the origin of that energy and provided the reader with techniques to recognize and connect to it. It lacked, however, a discussion of the forces that impact your perception of this energy. All persons and situations have an influence on your unique perspective and actions. Your individual perspective directs your interactions with the universal energy. Without understanding your perspective, your inner voice and your intuition will be interpreted by ego. As long as your intuition is heard by ego, obtaining lasting joy and peace will elude you as you are not truly manifesting your life purpose.

I loved the evolution of this book from one with a primary focus of duality to one with a focus on your inner voice and manifestation, for it is my belief that intuition and mediumship always begin with you. This evolution created dissonance within me as the title *Two* no longer felt right. When I hear the word "Two," images of two individual and unique objects immediately pop into my head. I picture two apples sitting on a table or a husband and wife. That is not what this book is about as we are one energy. Others may have an impact, but the growth in this book is internal and ultimately about you.

Weeks and months passed, and I struggled with the title. I had become wedded to the idea of *Two* and didn't want to walk away from the concept and title altogether. That is when the muses struck and *Two* became *Deux*. Deux, after all, is still "two," just in French. By changing the title to *Deux*, it continues the theme of numbers and signifies this is the follow-up to *One*. I loved the sound of *Deux* since the annunciation is similar to "you," which subconsciously suggests that ultimately the decision and trajectory of your life lies in your hands. My goal is to demonstrate that you, through choice, can manifest your hopes and desires.

While I loved the new title, I found others weren't convinced this was a wise move. In fact, after reviewing my manuscript one of my content editors strongly encouraged me to change the name of the book back to *Two* and she presented a number of good arguments to change it back. She contended that, "*some people might not know that deux means two*" and *"it could impact sales as people will be looking for Two."* Despite her recommendations, in my heart I was (and am) convinced that *Deux* is the fitting title.

I also could have also been dissuaded when my copy editor upon first hearing the change in name informed me that I was mispronouncing deux. I was aware and am doing it deliberately, as I mentioned I enjoyed the annunciation being similar to "you." Aware of that, inspiration struck my copy editor while reviewing the manuscript. After it did, she asked if I knew that *dieu*, the French word for God, sounded to a non-native speaker strikingly close to *deux*. I told her I didn't, but as it struck her it also struck me that this is why *Deux* was indeed the title of this book. Intuition is about God and God resides in every thing and every one. In *Deux*, we are exploring the God that resides within you. The universe inspires, even when an individual (like me) doesn't realize it.

As you read this book, you will find my personal stories. This is a result of the feedback I received from *One*. Many indicated that they loved the examples I used, for they spoke to their own experiences, but readers had hoped to hear more of my story. At first, I dismissed these comments and directed readers to my Blog, www.lifeofamedium.com, since over the years, I have shared stories of my life and my experiences there. In writing *Deux*, I found that sharing my story was appropriate because it demonstrates an environment supportive of the development of intuition that allowed me to grow into the medium I am today and, more importantly, to live a life filled with joy and fulfillment. As I tell my story, don't be surprised if you read my experiences and think, *"Wow! That happened to me too!"* I say that with confidence because I know my life isn't that different from yours and it demonstrates the universal elements. By understanding them, you will be able not only to develop your intuition and understand your inner voice but also manifest your heart's desires. I hope this book provides you with insight that sets you on a path towards intuition, your life purpose and the joy found when you are aligned with your soul.

SECTION ONE
KNOW YOUR STORY

CHAPTER ONE
ENERGY EXPANDED

"If connection is the energy that surges between people, we have to remember that those surges must travel in both directions."
Brené Brown

A universal energy exists around and within each animate and inanimate being on our planet and beyond. The vibrations continuously emitted by all living and inanimate beings create the world you perceive consciously with your five senses – sight, sound, sensation, taste and smell. Not only that, those vibrations connect you to the energy matrix that is indistinguishable to the naked eye yet perceived by your sixth sense. This matrix of energy has a significant impact on you whether you are aware of and actively engaging with it or not. The magnitude of this invisible energy is demonstrated by the moon's pull on the earth, which creates the tides, an infant's cry that causes a nursing mother's nipples to release milk, and the heckles shouted by a fan that cause an athlete to have a false start. These energetic connections are unseen yet have a physical, mental, emotional and spiritual impact on every individual.

Many are ignorant of these unseen energetic connections and go through life without an awareness that the energy emitted and received impacts them on a day-to-day, moment-to-moment basis. Further, without this awareness many go through life in opposition to the energy around them which, at best, creates more work for the individual and, at worst, creates distress. Think of it in terms of hairstyles. Imagine you have thick, curly hair. You go to the stylist and ask for a style tailored for straight hair. The stylist informs you that while he or she can cut your hair to the desired look, the style will require straightening and product without which your hair will turn into a frizzy mess. If you agree, every day you will spend a great deal of time maintaining the chosen style, whereas a style designed for curls will save you time and energy. Without an awareness of your hair type, you don't have the information to make an informed decision. Not being aware of the energetic connections around you is like not having an awareness of your hair type.

Not being aware makes it difficult to formulate an informed decision not only because you don't have the facts to facilitate a decision, but you also remain ignorant to the potential solutions and tools that could make your life easier. Think of it in terms of eyesight. Imagine that for your entire life everything you have seen is blurry. You may assume that this is typical and are unaware that there are tools, such as glasses, that could sharpen your vision. Without the tool, the glasses, you stumble through life. Whether it's the ill-chosen hairstyle or the blurry vision, each situation creates challenges. The same can be said of one's ignorance of energetic connections.

These energetic connections are the building blocks of intuition. Intuition occurs when an individual is aware and responds to those energetic connections. Consider this: intuition is like baking a cake. You can have flour, sugar, eggs, all the ingredients that go into a cake yet not have a cake. The ingredients, like the energetic connections around you, are just components. If you have all the ingredients but don't have or know how to follow a recipe, you will not have a cake. Similarly, even if you are aware of the energetic connections but don't know how to interpret them, your intuition will elude you. It's not until the ingredients are measured and mixed, put in the oven, and baked for a specific length of time at a specific temperature that you have a cake. Intuition works the same way. Until you quiet your mind, put your ego aside and are objective in your interpretation, your intuition will be shaky and perhaps misguide you. Once you listen to your inner voice, manifesting your heart's desires is like sitting down and eating the cake.

Unfortunately, putting the ego aside and being objective is easier said than done. In fact, putting the ego aside will be a lifelong endeavor since every action impacts the journey. Each situation, as indicated, is energy and as such is governed by the laws of nature. This includes Newton's Third Law of Motion: "*For every action there is an equal and opposite reaction.*" This law is demonstrated in that situations that occur to an individual impact that individual's future behavior. The future behavior may be immediate, or it could occur in the distant future. The resulting behavior may be an isolated occurrence, or it could become perpetual. The nature of the response will be determined by a multitude of factors.

Fortunately, just as in a game of pinball, you have within your control the ability to direct your response to any given situation. This begins by being aware of the energies that are impacting you. Let's liken intuition to archery. An individual's innate ability is the arrow itself. Arrows are made from a variety of materials. Some of those materials are heavier, others are lighter. Some of these materials are sleeker and hence more aerodynamic. And some are designed to go farther and straighter and will go farther regardless of the archer's skill. Unlike the archer, you don't get to choose your arrow. You are born with innate, biological abilities and tendencies towards intuition. Because of this, there are individuals who are naturally more intuitive than others. You may be one of those people, you may not. Fortunately, just as an individual dedicated to archery learns to shoot an arrow, an individual dedicated to enhancing his or her intuition will become intuitive.

An innate tendency is only a very small factor in an individual's intuitive ability. Like the archer, many other factors influence an individual on any given day. For example, the archer must consider his or her environment. On the day of a competition, the archer could face wind, rain, sun, even snow. That environment is going to impact the archer's ability to perform. The wind will affect the trajectory of the arrow, whereas the rain or snow could weigh the arrow down and limit the distance it travels; even the sun could cause challenges if it happens to be blinding. To be successful, the archer must take these environmental factors into consideration. Similarly, to enhance one's intuition an individual should consider his or her environment. An individual's environment includes factors such as culture, community and religion. In addition to one's environment, the individuals a blossoming intuitive encounters influence his or her perspective as well. Likening this to the archer, the individuals in the seeker's life are akin to the fans and the naysayers, even the coach, teammates and rivals. The opinions of these individuals may impact the archer's opinion of his or her own skill, and as a result, his or her performance. For example, if the archer is surrounded by onlookers sitting in hushed and reverent anticipation, the archer may perform better than in front of a crowd that is loud or booing. The crowd serves as a metaphor for an individual's social network, family, friends, classmates and colleagues. Finally, and perhaps most importantly, an aspiring intuitive is impacted by his or her history. In terms of the archer, if the archer is on a winning spree, he or she may perform better than if he or she has hit a losing streak. Similarly, if the archer has never won at a given venue, that may affect his or her performance. The same can be said of an individual's experiences and subsequent ego.

It is apparent that these factors, both nature and nurture, affect the archer both positively and negatively. The factors in and of themselves are not good or bad; they are just the landscape through which the archer must navigate. In fact, the perceived handicaps can be overcome and managed by the archer's dedication to and practice of his or her sport. The same is true of a developing intuitive. One's current circumstances do not define or limit his or her future. Rather, it is an individual's dedication and persistence that define his or her future. As with the archer, a skilled athlete has spent hours in practice. He or she has trained in the rain, wind, sun and even snow. Through this he or she has learned the effect the weather has on the direction of the arrow and, more importantly, how to tweak his or her execution to accommodate for the given conditions. He or she has practiced in both quiet and loud environments. In doing so, he or she has learned how to shut the noise out and become one with the arrow, much like an intuitive who becomes one with the universe despite external factors. Due to this preparation no matter what the environment, the skilled archer will hit the target almost every time. The same can be said of an intuitive. Once an individual has identified the energies influencing him or her and the impact these factors have, he or she can choose to adapt his or her behavior to obtain a different outcome. By adjusting one's behavior, the individual becomes an active participant in his or her life and can manifest his or her heart's desires.

Sounds amazing, doesn't it? It is. But it isn't easy. To do this, you must recognize and accept your unique set of distractions and limitations. Unfortunately, unlike in archery, where the archer through observation can deduce the effect of the environment, in intuition the obstacles impacting you lie beneath the surface and may be deeply ingrained within you and your belief system. Again, consider the archer. If he or she questions his or her ability, the heckler will have a much greater impact than an archer with confidence in his or her ability. At the end of the day it isn't the words the heckler is shouting, it is the interpretation and feelings the commentary elicits in the archer. With that in mind, for your intuition to flourish you must be able to ignore the hecklers. The first step in doing this is to become comfortable in your own skin. You cannot be comfortable in your own skin if you don't know your story and understand the driving forces behind your actions. Without understanding your motivations, you are like an affluent individual pretending to be impoverished. An individual who has always had wealth is unable to comprehend and conceive of the challenges poor individuals encounter daily. To understand your motivations, as you delve into your past you are encouraged to behave like an actor preparing for his or her new role. An actor prepares for a part by imagining or living life through the eyes of his or her character. While preparing, the actor not only visualizes the character's own behaviors but also the interactions the character has with those he or she encounters, for the manner in which others respond to an individual is important since it informs one's response to a situation. By applying this technique, you will begin to understand your actions, motivations and belief system. With this awareness, you will have the choice to release behaviors that do not serve you. In doing so, you will find your intuition flows effortlessly as you will no longer be hindered by fear or belief systems that are in opposition to your goals. Not sure what I mean? Visualize the following. Your intuition flows through you like water flows through a pipe. Experiences such as being told your imaginary friend wasn't real or that you shouldn't consult a medium to contact your deceased loved ones are particles that get stuck in that pipe. Some of these particles are bigger than others, but over a lifetime even the smallest particles add up. Like a sink's drain, it is not until the pipe is clogged and water doesn't drain that you recognize the impact of all those small particles such as hair and toothpaste. Yet the pipes are clogging up long before there is a problem.

Like the pipes of a sink, everyone has gunk in their pipes of intuition. As you endeavor on your quest to enhance your awareness, it is important to clean your pipes because the gunk slows your intuition. The energies that are in opposition to your life purpose create the gunk. When you go through the process of understanding your story and releasing that which does not serve you, you are figuratively pouring drain cleaner down the pipe. Once the pipe is cleared, your intuition, like the water, flows more smoothly.

Once your intuition is flowing, your inner voice and life's purpose become apparent. With your hopes and dreams visible, you can easily step in as protagonist in your story as opposed to the sidekick. Where you once reflexively responded to the actions of individuals in your life and your environment, you will find you now respond consciously, always taking steps towards your desires and life's purpose. Additionally, you will become more aware of the synchronicities in your life that provide you opportunities to further your goals.

Being aware of the synchronicities occurring in your life and not defined by anyone's expectations except your own, you can choose not only to be the protagonist of your story but also the author. A gift bestowed upon us by creator is free will, which means you can write your own story. In doing so you are not a passive recipient of gifts or hardships. Rather, the things you manifest, good and bad, are consequences of your own choices. As suggested, you may experience hardship and strife as a result of those choices, but since that discomfort is of your own choosing, it is usually short-lived, manageable and ultimately brings you closer to your purpose.

Let's explore an example of this. As a child while playing the game *Would You Rather* and faced with the question, *"Would you rather be deaf or blind?"*, I always, without hesitation, opted for blind. When asked for a reason, my response was always that I couldn't imagine a world without music. I was a musician and found music could instantly change my mood for the better. Art, such as paintings and drawings, never brought me the same joy. I'd go to an art museum and walk away thinking, *"I don't get it."* Ironically, after a car accident, I was left legally blind. I often wonder if playing *Would You Rather* was the universe's way of prompting a choice and what the outcome would have been had I chosen being deaf.

Let's explore the example of my loss of sight further. Despite the hardships it creates, including the inability to drive, I've also considered myself blessed that it was my vision and not my hearing that went. The loss of sight is manageable, as noted, but I can't imagine a world without sound. Additionally, I know that my loss of vision has furthered the development of my intuition. Without peripheral sight, I was forced to become more attuned to the energy around me. Being attuned to the energies around me has been vital in navigating my environment.

Before you can become the author of your story, even unwittingly, as in the example of my sight, you first need to understand your story. Let's get started.

CHAPTER TWO
GENETICS

"I think I was dealt a good hand. I have happy genes."
Maeve Binchy

Reflecting on the cake metaphor described in chapter one, an individual is unable to bake a cake if he or she lacks ingredients which dictate the type of cake that will be made. For example, if an individual has an abundance of carrots, he or she may choose to prepare a carrot cake, whereas if the individual finds a liquor cabinet full of rum, he or she may opt to make a rum cake. Just as the ingredients available to a baker directs the type of cake he or she will bake, one's genetic make-up directs one's intuitive development. As a result, the logical place to begin the discussion of your intuitive development and ability to manifest begins with your innate abilities.

Science has demonstrated that personality traits, talents and behaviors are a result, at least in part, of genetic predisposition. Although one doesn't need science to tell us that, the role genetics plays in inherited abilities is witnessed through anecdotal observation. Take for example the Manning family. A father and three brothers have all demonstrated skill and experienced success in playing football. Observing these men, one may deduce that a natural, athletic predisposition exists in their family. Not only have these men been recruited to play football professionally, multiple Superbowl rings have been obtained. That doesn't convince you? Consider Irene Joloit-Curie, daughter of Marie and Pierre Curie. She, like her parents, was awarded a Nobel Prize. From this, one could deduce she inherited intelligence and an inclination towards science from her parents. By simply observing families, it becomes apparent abilities have a genetic predisposition.

While the Mannings and Curies illustrate that athleticism and intelligence run in families, a belief exists that intuition is an inherited trait as well. Many psychics and mediums bank upon the commonly held belief that intuition is inherited and tout being a generational intuitive. As there is no way currently to credential a medium, this terminology offers the psychic or medium credibility. For some, it is believed a long lineage means that individual is blessed with a stronger ability. There may be some truth in this belief as most of the psychics and mediums I have encountered do come from a family with a rich history of intuitive gifts, myself included. Additionally, research has demonstrated that empathy, a form of intuition, does have a genetic component.

Let's explore that genetic component by using my family as an example. In my family, intuitive abilities and mediumship can be traced back four generations on my maternal side with a lineage that begins with my mother's great uncle, Norman Mootz. He was my grandfather's uncle as well as a medium and Spiritualist Minister.

Born around the turn of the twentieth century, Norm was part of the Spiritualist heyday. Spiritualism as a religion promotes the belief that life is eternal and as a result the soul or spirit exists beyond death. More than that, Spiritualists believe that on the earth plane we have the ability to communicate with souls that exist on the spiritual plane. This belief system was popular in the late 1800s and early 1900s when Norman was alive as families suffered and grieved the loved ones lost in the Civil War and World War I. Norman was no different. He was drawn to Spiritualism and as a result spent many summers in Lily Dale, a Spiritualist Camp located in southwest New York. His affiliation with the community is evidenced by two concrete slabs that comprise the patio surrounding Inspiration Stump, one for Rev. & Mrs. Norman Mootz and the other for Norman's only child, Eugene.

My grandfather, Albert, benefited from his uncle's affiliation. After Al lost his mother as a child, Norm took his nephew under his wing. Through Norm, Al was introduced to Spiritualism, Lily Dale and mediumship. While my grandfather never became a practicing medium, his connection with spirit assisted him in grieving his mother and enriched his life.

Al passed when I was eleven, so I never had the opportunity to ask my grandfather if he had a desire to become a professional medium, but if he did it was not a practical career path. He and my grandmother, Lois, had seven children. With many mouths to feed, he found work at the local steel mill.

Al was not a professional medium. In fact, from outside appearances, Al appeared to be the farthest thing from it. He was rough around the edges, cursed, held deeply rooted prejudices, and had a volatile personality. Despite that, he lived his life with a strong faith, saw ghosts everywhere he went and was intuitive. His faith and belief in life after death were instilled in my mother and her siblings. My mother has commented on numerous occasions that her parents would tell her and her siblings, *"Don't worry you'll never be alone, when I die, I'll come back and visit you."*

Her mother told her this as much as her father. The need to reassure the children that they have the ability and would visit from beyond the grave may seem morbid, it may also have been intuition. In April 1971 tragedy struck the family. That April, the family homestead caught fire. My grandmother and three of the children didn't make it out alive. Their loss devastated my grandfather. His temper flared, he drank (more) and began to spiral out of control. Fortunately, Norm's son Eugene stepped in. Like his father, Gene assisted my grandfather in dealing with his grief. He reminded my grandfather that he could use mediumship as a coping mechanism for his grief. Al did just that and from that point in his life on, he would see more spirits in an establishment than living people. The dead brought him comfort that the living could not.

Mediumship didn't skip a generation and go directly from my grandfather to me. Of the four remaining children, none would call themselves mediums. I would. They have all shared experiences that I define as mediumship or at the very least spiritual encounters: the eldest, a collector of cuckoo clocks, found that the clocks in his home chirped at random, usually accompanied by a cold breeze; my aunt speaks of a man who appeared at the end of her bed and scared her to the point that she slept with the light on for months; my mother knows my grandfather is visiting as she feels his presence and smells smoke; and, the youngest shared an experience he had where after praying for a visit from his mom he saw her appear clear as day in a mirror. For some in my mother's generation, these experiences occur frequently; for others the experiences are sporadic. Their perception of these occurrences varies, person to person and moment to moment. At times they are afraid. Sometimes they are skeptical. At other points they yearn for more understanding. And, at other points they have no interest in being able to do what I do. As a result, my mom and her siblings remain passive receivers and instead of honing their gifts; whenever they get an inkling that a deceased loved one wants to talk, they get a reading from a professional medium.

That brings us to my generation. As one of eleven grandchildren, I'm the only one that has actively pursued the development of mediumship. While I may be the only "medium" in the family, all of my grandfather's grandchildren I am in contact with have shared experiences that I would classify as intuitive experiences. For example, one cousin recounts her discomfort regarding a corner of her bedroom. That is the same corner where I have seen a spirit visit. Another cousin has shared that the radio inexplicably turns on and plays one of her father's favorite songs whenever she is thinking about him. The stories are numerous and account for nine of the eleven. The two remaining I assume have had experiences, but I cannot say for sure. Those I am in contact with are like my mom and her siblings: they have an ability but choose not to utilize or develop it.

At this point it should be apparent that mediumship is an ability that runs in my family. Anecdotally, this supports the theory that individuals can be genetically predisposed to intuition. If it does, a predisposition will assist your development. Take a moment to reflect on your family tree and your potential predisposition to intuition.

Questions to Consider

Do you have relatives that are mediums, psychics, tea leaf or tarot readers, or something else?

> *Have your relatives expressed experiences that lead you to believe they have had communication with deceased loved ones either through visions, signs or dreams?*
>
> *Has your mother, father, siblings or grandparents had an experience in which they have seen a ghost? If they have, was it once or on numerous occasions?*
>
> *Have experiences like these occurred to numerous people in your family?*

If you answered yes to any of these questions, intuition is in your family. The more frequently these occurred, the stronger it is. If you didn't answer yes to any of these questions or they haven't occurred frequently, don't assume a predisposition to intuition doesn't exist. The questions posed only addressed experiences considered mediumship, the ability to feel and communicate with deceased loved ones. Mediumship is only a very small part of intuition! Let's continue the conversation and turn to the broader topic of intuition.

Intuition as defined in this book is an instinctive knowing that comes from being observant of your environment using your five senses and being aware of your gut feelings or knowing as provided through your sixth sense. Intuition may present itself through the synchronicities one experiences, the inexplicable messages one gets, or the connection one feels to the environment and the individuals within it. If you haven't experienced encounters with deceased loved ones, chances are you have had one of the following intuitive experiences:

Stroke of Luck: Are you like my uncle who has a knack of knowing when to go to a casino and once there knows what slots or tables to play? My uncle listens to his intuition and he always wins. Sometimes it's a lot, sometimes it isn't. The same may be true for you. You might win on scratch offs or you may always win the door prize. If you find yourself touched by luck, it may just be your intuition!

Dreams: Do you have intuitive dreams like my cousin? Prior to my husband and me announcing our pregnancy, she had a vivid dream of me pregnant with a little girl. At the time, we hadn't informed anyone that we were taking a few months to "see what happened" and publicly we maintained that we weren't having kids. Despite that, she was convinced that a pregnancy was on the horizon and shared the dream with her mother a couple weeks before we were even pregnant. If you find yourself having precognitive dreams, this is a sign of intuition.

Inner Knowing: Are you like my mom who always knows who is calling? Before caller id, my mom always knew who was on the line, sometimes before the phone even rang. Or perhaps you think about someone and then bump into them. What about purchasing an item at the grocery store because you feel compelled but don't know why? For example, I was contemplating getting my daughter a superhero costume. Before I had the chance to order it, my mom already had it ordered and delivered. If situations like these occur to you, intuition is at play.

Right Place, Right Time: Do you tend to find yourself in the right place at the right time? My husband and I do. A great example is when we bumped into a comedian we were going to see at dinner prior to the performance. It was at a restaurant we don't typically frequent, but we were in the right place at the right time and were blessed to meet the funny man personally. Again, intuition was working.

Intuitive individuals have experiences like those just described because they are more attuned to the energies that connect each of us. Aware of those energies, even at a subconscious level, individuals respond to their environment in a manner that is in resonance with the energies, and as a result the individuals have rewarding experiences. These individuals' actions are directed through their heart and an internal knowing as opposed to through reasoning and intellect. Their actions are rarely based on immediate gratification or what they have been told to do, but rather because they feel it is the "right" thing. They trust their instincts on a physical, emotional and spiritual level and, most importantly, regularly choose to act upon the information they have received.

Intuition appears in many forms, but the commonality is that intuitives are led by their gut feelings, not their heads. Intuition can manifest itself through athletics, counseling or even accounting. For example, a natural athlete has the skill for throwing a basketball, the intuitive athlete pays attention to all the players and knows when to dart to the left or right to avoid another player and places him or herself in position to score a goal. Similarly, the individual with a natural affinity math may go into finance and have success in banking, while the intuitive may have great success on Wall Street by paying attention to the trends and intuiting when to take a risk and invest in a new company or quickly pull money out of a company. I enjoy listening to my intuition while shopping and as a result have a knack for finding amazing deals. For example, I recently purchased a stunning dress.

I eyed it while Christmas shopping with a friend, noticed it was thirty percent off and tried it on. Despite a perfect fit, I opted not to purchase. The next day I couldn't get the dress out of my head and decided I would buy the dress. Before heading to the store, I found two coupons: one for an additional twenty percent off any sale item, the other for ten dollars off any purchase of thirty dollars or more. The coupons did not indicate they could not be used together. At the register, I handed the cashier the coupons, when both coupons were applied to the sale it brought the dress to the price I had been hoping to pay the night before. Had I purchased the dress when I first eyed it, I wouldn't have gotten these deals and paid more than I wanted to. In this example, not only had my intuition stalled the purchase, it also alerted me to the coupons I had forgotten in my purse and the price of the dress. Examples like these demonstrate that intuition will touch every aspect of your life if you allow it to.

Consider the various intuitive examples just discussed and take a moment to reflect on the intuitive incidents you and your relatives have experienced.

Questions to Consider

Have you had episodes of intuition? Do your family members have episodes of intuition? If so, how often?

Of your intuitive experiences what occurs most frequently? What about for your relatives?

Does intuition manifest in you or your family another way? If so, how?

When intuition strikes, do you listen? If so, are the outcomes rewarding?

When you reflect on these questions, if you find that these occurrences happen sometimes or often, your intuition is higher than normal and if they happen to your family, you are predisposed. At this point, it is likely you have found you are predisposed to intuition. But if your perception is that you and your family never have any of these experiences and you are concerned that you don't have the right ingredients, I guarantee you do. Your natural inclination towards intuition is evidenced by the fact you chose to read this book. Individuals gravitate towards subjects, hobbies and topics they have a natural inclination towards as we have a desire to be successful in our endeavors. If you weren't predisposed, you would have left the book on the book shelf or would have put it down after the reading the first page.

Still not convinced? That's okay. Let's assume you don't have an innate ability for intuition. It doesn't matter. Ultimately to be intuitive you need only one thing – to be alive. That's it. While other factors play a role and bolster your intuition, being alive is all you need. As already discussed, it is your living, breathing soul that creates a connection with the universe and that connection will facilitate intuition. The other necessary factor to improve your intuition is a desire to do so, which reading this book demonstrates. Genetic predisposition is unnecessary; it just makes accessing your intuition easier. Not sure what I mean? Let's compare a naturally intuitive individual to one riding a motorcycle and one without a strong disposition to one driving a moped. If you own a moped, you know the vehicle won't go as fast as a motorcycle. In fact, it can be dangerous if you expect it to. As a result, it will always take you a little longer to get to your desired location. Additionally, because the moped is limited in its speed, you may not be able to take the fastest route via a well-maintained highway. Instead you may find yourself confined to taking a pot-hole laden back road. This road may not only result in a slower, but also a bumpier ride. Despite the challenges, the moped will ultimately get you to where you want to go. This is true of intuition as well. If you aren't naturally inclined to intuition it may take you a little longer to recognize and create the energetic connections, but you will get there.

Penny is an example of an individual with a weak predisposition to intuition. She comes from a family that looks at the world in terms of black or white. Valuing justice, she opted for a career in law. Being an incredibly compassionate individual, she has elected to serve as an attorney for underprivileged individuals. According to Penny, her family never spoke about intuition or the paranormal during her childhood. In fact, she cannot recall ever having an "imaginary" friend, precognitive dream or visit from a deceased loved one.

For the first part of her adulthood, Penny didn't consider the paranormal and like her family dismissed it as a bunch of hooey. After her sister passed, that feeling changed. She missed her sister and began to ponder the afterlife hoping they would be reunited in the future. Around the same time, enthusiasm for her work also began to wane. Despite doubting her ability, discontent in her life created an insatiable yearning for connection. This desire brought her to intuitive development classes.

A dutiful student, Penny committed herself to the development of her intuition. Following each class, she took the lessons and applied them to her life. Despite her commitment, she struggled to connect to her intuition and upon reflection she doubted she had any natural inclination. She didn't give up. Penny was determined to overcome her perceived handicap as she wholeheartedly believed intuition would bring her peace. Unwaveringly she prayed, meditated, practiced all the techniques suggested by teachers and peers, and enjoyed the community she found. Then after years of practice, without any apparent reason, her intuition started flowing. When it did, she understood the insatiable desire she had all along WAS her intuition. It had been with her all along.

You may feel like Penny. You may feel you haven't got what it takes. Penny had what it takes, and you do too. Penny demonstrates that while genetic predisposition plays a role, it is only a very small part of the intuition equation. In fact, being genetically predisposed does not mean that intuition will naturally present itself. One can be genetically predisposed, but because of external influences, be closed-minded and unaware of the energy that is impacting him or her. Think of it in terms of genetic conditions such as breast cancer. Researchers have proven that mutations to a specific gene, BRCA1, is linked to the development of breast cancer. Individuals with this specific mutation are more likely to develop breast or ovarian cancer, but there is also the chance they won't. Just because the individual is born with the mutation does not mean that the individual is destined to develop cancer. Similarly, an individual without the mutation cannot assume he or she will not develop breast cancer. While the likelihood may be lower, it doesn't mean he or she is in the clear. Rather, one's genetics are only a fraction of the equation. In fact, one's lifestyle choices and environment are stronger predictors. Similarly, an individual's lifestyle, environment, peers and desire to connect with the universe play a larger role in the development of one's intuition than genetics. Penny illustrated this. She is an individual who did not consider herself genetically predisposed, despite that she awakened her intuition through her own determination. You can too.

CHAPTER THREE
PARENTS & CAREGIVERS

"Parents are the ultimate role models for children. Every word, movement and action has an effect. No other person or outside force has a greater influence on a child than a parent."
Bob Keeshan

Nature, as discussed in the previous chapter, influences one's intuition. In the next several chapters, nurture or the impact experiences have on an individual, will be explored and you will be encouraged to embark on a journey of self-reflection. As you are reading these chapters, you may wonder why, in a book about intuition, you are spending time reflecting on your past experiences. The reason is simple. Ego is the number one obstacle individuals face in their intuitive pursuits, and one's ego is created by past experiences, good and bad. Self-reflection provides significant insight into an individual's history and the perspective by which he or she views the world. With an understanding of one's perspective, an individual will more clearly interpret his or her intuition.

Albert Bandura first demonstrated how impressionable individuals, specifically children, are in the 1960s. In his experiment he observed children exhibiting behaviors they had moments before witnessed an adult portraying. Bandura's experiment has been replicated by researchers on numerous occasions. To see more evidence of this experiment, you needn't look any further than a small child in your life and my daughter is a classic example. To preface this story, I will share that my husband would tell you I'm a "neat freak." I would counter and tell you I dislike disorganization. As you can imagine, maintaining a clutter-free home with a toddler is challenging, but I tried. To minimize the disorder, while playing with my daughter, I straightened up behind her. When she finished playing with a puzzle, I put the remaining pieces in place as she played with her blocks. When she was done with her blocks and moved on to coloring, I'd neatly stack the blocks. I'd do this without saying a word. I didn't call her messy or comment on the disarray as I was aware that my preference would impact her and didn't want her to see playing and the consequent clutter negatively. Instead, the interactions we had as I straightened up revolved around whatever activity she was engaged in presently. I'd tell her, *"Good job stacking those blocks"* or *"That's a beautiful picture you are making."* I just happened to be tidying up as well. Despite that, my daughter's observations resulted in, without instruction, her picking up after herself. She observed the behavior and adopted it as her own, which supports the theory of nurtured behavior.

Adopting the behavior demonstrates that parents' actions do have an impact on their children's actions. You may be thinking, *"Big deal! In the grand scheme of life, what does this matter?"* In a situation like the one discussed above, it doesn't matter. Tidiness, while a virtue, is relatively insignificant. The adoption of other behaviors, such as drug and physical abuse, are more significant and unsavory. In either case, the impact of the observation and adoption of behaviors goes beyond a simple mimicking of said behavior, and that is where the influence is truly instrumental. Let's delve further into the story.

Hattie, my daughter's friend, came over to play one day. She is a little younger than my daughter and a lot more active. Due to her activity and propensity to scatter toys, the little girl's parents nicknamed her "Hurricane Hattie." While the girls were playing, both in typical fashion – Hattie being a Hurricane and my daughter playing with an item and then neatly putting it away, I overheard my daughter comment with annoyance that Hattie was "messy" as she scrambled to pick up and restack the blocks her friend had just scattered all over the room. The annoyance in my daughter's voice indicated that her friend's behavior was not in alignment with her values. If this had been an isolated occurrence, it could have been interpreted that the annoyance was because Hattie knocking over the blocks had disrupted a tower or castle my daughter was building. Her response on the following St. Patrick's Day indicated that was not the case. Holidays, no matter how small, are a big deal in my home. On St Patrick's Day, my husband and I thought it would be fun for our daughter to wake up to leprechaun mayhem. We staged the house to appear as though leprechauns had visited overnight, spilling cereal, creating a trap, and leaving footprints, chocolate coins and balloons all around the home. Rather than enjoying the mischief, my daughter's first response was, *"Eh.. we need to clean up this mess."*

In these two examples, my daughter's attitude and displeasure demonstrate that not only had she embraced the habit of cleaning up after herself, she created a belief system that values tidiness around the adopted behaviors. Not impressed? She was two and a half! If you have been around many toddlers, you know the value my daughter places on tidiness is atypical. Additionally, one can assume she did not have an innate desire for tidiness; rather, as she mimicked my actions, she internalized my belief system as her own.

The adoption of behaviors and belief systems as demonstrated by my daughter's desire for neatness, begin at very young age. Some psychologists believe the environmental impact parents have on their children begins as early as conception. Providers who ascribe to this belief system encourage expectant mothers and fathers to read, play music and converse with the unborn child. If you do not ascribe to this belief, we can all agree that from the moment of birth the environment begins to impact the child. At this young age, the child is incapable of comprehending the influence conditions have on him or her and as a result is a passive participant in his or her life. The adoption of these beliefs is for the purpose of survival more than conscious awareness. For example, my daughter and I didn't have a conversation about the benefits of being organized, she didn't consciously decide that tidiness is a trait she would value; instead, she witnessed my behavior and belief system and passively adopted it as her own.

These early belief systems become the foundation of an individual's identity. For example, a child born into a family that enjoys athletics may provide the infant with toys such as balls, bats and mitts. As that child grows, he or she may be enrolled in sports programs and be taken to sporting events. Similarly, a family that is musically inclined instead of giving toys such as bats and balls may provide his or her child with rattles, drums and tambourines and enroll the child in music programs. The introduction of interests and activities early in life will impact the interests a child has later in life. The child introduced to athletics is more likely to enjoy sports throughout his or her life, whereas the child introduced to music will more likely enjoy music throughout his or her life. This occurs for a multitude of reasons. Neurologically, a child's brain is being programmed to perform the specific activities. For example, scientists encourage children be introduced to foreign languages at an early age due to the plasticity of their brains; it is easier for the child to learn the language not only as a child but as an adult as well. Additionally, the earlier a child is exposed to an interest, the earlier he or she begins to develop a proficiency. For example, a child that has been playing piano for three years due simply to his or her exposure will perform better than a child of the same age that started a week ago. The exposure and subsequent skill will impact his or her opinion of it positively. If a child's perspective is that he or she is "better" at a task, it is more likely that he or she will continue that activity. The third and final reason is that a child has an innate desire to please the adults in his or her life. If he or she sees the activities delight the adults around him or her, he or she is more likely to enjoy the activities presented.

The parents' influence on their children's likes and dislikes is often done unintentionally, and in many cases with good intention. I cleaned up after my daughter to give her room to play and ensure toys weren't lost. Parents enroll their children in programs because they want their children's lives to be enriched. Despite that, these actions have an impact, an impact that is neither good nor bad, it just is. Awareness of that influence is important in your quest toward intuition and your life purpose because the belief system within which you operate affects your choices and your selections reaffirm the belief system you live within. Not only do children unconsciously adopt and create value systems around observed behaviors, they create belief systems around circumstances they don't know based on the facts they are aware of!

The examples discussed above demonstrate how parent's deliberate and unintentional actions impact a child. Just as my husband and I are shaping our daughter, my parents affected me, your parents molded you, you have impacted children in your life, our children will influence children in their lives, so forth and so on. It is a natural and never-ending cycle.

As mentioned earlier, this unending cycle is not bad, it just is. The behaviors and resulting beliefs that are intentionally and unintentionally instilled in you by your parents create a foundation of who you are today and should be respected. Are you honoring that foundation? Few people do. In fact, few people even recognize the belief systems their parents ingrained within them. I know I didn't. For example, while growing up I was told I was a terrible eater. My mother would reiterate how she dreaded feeding me as an infant. She recounted how it would take three hours to feed me, and since the recommendation was to feed a child every three hours from the beginning of a feeding, she was feeding me nonstop which was exhausting.

I heard that story I don't know how many times in my life, especially since the fussiness for food continued throughout my childhood, young adulthood and is the biggest challenge my husband and I have today. Hearing the story and the tone my mother used when retelling it, I assumed I was somehow to blame. Recently, the guilt I carried regarding food was lifted. While nursing my daughter, my mother made this eye-opening comment, *"Your daughter is such a good eater and so healthy. I wonder what would have happened had I nursed you. We must have tried a dozen different formulas before we found one you could stomach; you threw the rest up."* It was an a-ha moment. I didn't know I suffered reflux, had food sensitivities and couldn't keep formulas down. With that information, a sense of relief set in, and I no longer felt guilt for my food issues. Instead, I understood my issues likely began as that infant who was sick every time I ate. Still, having been told I was a terrible eater, that is what I became.

Like this, all our actions and beliefs have a root source. Finding that root is hard work and will take a lifetime, and even then, you won't have found the root for all your behaviors and beliefs. However, starting to do that work is a big step in unleashing your intuition and a bigger step in manifesting your heart's desires because you will no longer be limited by the beliefs and desires others have imprinted on you. It's important to remember that finding the root source is only the first step. After finding the root cause, you must work to modify your habits toward ones that assist in the manifestation of your hopes and dreams. Finding the root source, nonetheless, is a huge first step.

Let's begin to explore the belief systems imprinted upon you by your parents and/or caregivers. You could delve into all your belief systems and dissect each, one by one, to get a greater understanding of yourself. That's not necessarily a bad thing, but it's a much larger and time-consuming endeavor than what is intended by this book. As I mentioned, it could take a lifetime! Since this book is about intuition and manifestation of your life purpose, let's limit today's exploration to your parents' attitudes towards intuition and the hopes and dreams you expressed as a child. As we explore these attitudes, make note how they may have supported or hindered your intuition and beliefs and the influence these attitudes have on your behaviors today.

I was fortunate; I know that my parents' attitudes supported my development as they nurtured my confidence and individuality. In terms of spiritual matters, growing up we spoke of the existence of life after death and the ability for loved ones to come and visit after they had died. We watched movies like *Ghost, All Dogs Go* to Heaven, *Ghost Dad* and *Beetlejuice*. We believed in and watched for signs such as a bird flying into a window which meant someone was going to die or the number 11:11 which meant good luck. Being raised in an era prior to caller id, we made a game of guessing who was calling when the phone rang. I had a Ouija Board and deck of Tarot Cards. My dad purchased cassette tapes to hypnotize himself in hopes of losing weight. My mom saw mediums for readings. The paranormal was commonplace in my home.

Not only was the paranormal accepted, it was fully embraced. Every relative had a story of their experience with the spiritual realm. In fact, I was even given a story of my "first" experience before I could walk or talk. The story my mother tells occurred when I was about six months old. At that time, my aunt lived with my parents. All three caregivers changed my diapers, fed me, bathed me, and comforted me in my times of distress. Out of convenience, my nursery was situated between the master bedroom and my aunt's room at the other end of the hall. When I would be roused during the night, my mother or aunt would go in and coo me back to sleep.

The night of my experience was like any other night. I was put to bed, and several hours later I began fussing. Knowing that I would sometimes calm and soothe myself, both my aunt and mother stayed in bed listening intently. My mother recounts that after a few moments she heard a woman's voice offering soothing words. With those words, my fussiness subsided, and I began babbling right along with her. Grateful I was taken care of and she didn't have to get out of bed, my mother went back to sleep.

Over coffee the next morning, my mother thanked my aunt for attending to me the night before as she was exhausted and appreciated the sleep. Astonished, my aunt is said to exclaim, "*I wasn't in with the baby! I heard you talking to her, so I turned over and went back to sleep.*"

My mom and aunt were delighted I had my first experience with spirit and that it was a kind one. From that moment forward, they believed I was being watched by a guardian angel, whom they assumed was my grandmother. Even though I was too young to remember this occurrence, the experience has become part of my identity. Reflecting on the story, I see how this story supported several beliefs I developed as a young child. One, I was never afraid of being alone. I knew there were always family members around should I need help. As mentioned, as an infant I had not two, but three adults that attended to my needs. Even after my aunt moved out, she was still always around. If it wasn't one of my parents shuttling me to one of my many activities, it was my aunt. In addition to my aunt, my grandmother was also frequently a caregiver who lived with us on and off throughout my childhood. Finally, it was impressed upon me that I was also being watched by a guardian angel. This story supported this belief, as did my grandfather's stories of our spirit guides. With all these loved ones, how could I be afraid of being alone? Help was only ever a call away. Another belief this experience supported was that just because you couldn't see something, didn't mean it didn't exist. Neither my mother nor my aunt saw the spirit, but they believed their experience and that there was always more than what meets the eye. My family always encouraged me to think outside the box and not be limited to my current understanding. Being able not only to have faith in the unknown but also being encouraged to leap into that unknown has truly been a blessing. Reflecting on my life, I believe this is the biggest factor that not only developed my intuition but that has also provided me with the ability to manifest positive outcomes in my life.

Let's now turn to your parents/caregivers and your experiences. The night my grandmother visited my room was accepted and embraced by my family. Imagine you were me, the crying infant, and your mother, father or other caregivers were the ones who heard you and subsequently heard the woman's voice in the nursery.

Questions to Consider

How do you believe your caregivers would have responded?

Would the response have been positive, negative or nonexistent?

How would your family have told the story? Would they have told the story?

What experiences have you had that lead you to believe your caregivers would respond in a particular manner? Do you have a similar story?

If you believe your family would have responded positively, you are one of the lucky ones. However, if you believe they would have ignored the situation or responded negatively, you aren't out of luck and you are far from alone. As a medium, I know that experiences like the one I described can be unnerving, especially if it is outside of an individual's experience. In any given year, I receive dozens of messages from clients requesting assistance due to fear of activity from unseen forces. For example, while writing this book I received an email from a gentleman asking what to do for his three-year-old son. The message began with the man's declaration that his son was possessed by a demon. His belief his son was possessed came from the following observations: 1) unnerved, the babysitter contacted him after witnessing the child have a conversation with someone she could not see; 2) the child began exhibiting odd bodily movements including grunting; 3) the area of the home that the boy exhibited aforementioned behaviors had become ice cold; and, 4) the boy's sleep was disrupted by nightmares. Knowing that demonic possession is extremely rare, I queried the father for additional information. The assessment led me to the following conclusion: the child was intuitive and likely interacting with kind spirits (loved ones or spirit guides) as these entities only appear when the parents are not home, which is an indication that the spirits are present for protective reasons. Additionally, upon hearing the child had taken to watching zombie and ghost movies, I believed the child was mimicking behaviors from that programming and this may also have been affecting his sleep.

 Unfortunately, due to the prevalence of entertainment fixated on the existence of demons and malicious spirits, when individuals have an experience they do not understand, they jump to the worst case scenario. Most, and I do mean most, situations do not require an exorcism. The presence of a truly malevolent entity is rare. Many do not like to hear that. The father who wrote asking for help was not happy with the assessment or the advice that followed. I get it. It can be scary. You may have noticed that I have spoken of my maternal lineage but have said little in reference to my father's. The reason is because unlike my maternal relatives who embrace intuition, my father had little exposure to the paranormal realm and intuition prior to meeting my mother. He was raised in an Irish Catholic home in Brooklyn. His mother had attended college in the 1940s and studied Chemistry. His father was an insurance salesman. My father attended a parochial elementary school and earned entry into

Brooklyn Technical Institute for high school. Prior to his relationship with my mother, the only exposure he had to the paranormal was when his sister saw a gypsy prior to her wedding. The gypsy insisted my aunt not marry her fiancé as she saw heartache for my aunt. Unfortunately, this heartache came to pass as less than two years into their marriage my aunt lost her husband to cancer.

With that limited exposure, it should come as no surprise that my father was uncomfortable with intuition and paranormal experiences. It should also come as no surprise that while my mother and aunt have a positive recollection of my first intuitive experience, my father's first impression was much different. As he was a sound sleeper, he didn't hear the woman in the nursery that night. Instead, his first experience with my exhibition of interaction with the paranormal occurred when I was between the age of two and three. When my father tells the story, he sets the stage by saying I was a restless sleeper prone to nightmares. These nightmares had been escalating for weeks before the night in question. According to him, that night I came rushing into my parents' bedroom creating a scene, to hear him tell it, straight out of the *The Exorcist*. My eyes were wide open. My arms flailed as I scampered between the two of them and let out several blood curdling screams. These screams were followed by frantic, hushed communication much of which was unintelligible. From what he could make out, I was frightened by a snake. He comments that he was certain at any moment my head was going to spin around, and I was going to levitate off the bed. Perhaps from his own fear, he recalls the room became frigid, causing the hair on the back of his neck to stand up. He says while he couldn't see what I saw, he is convinced something was in the room with us that night. He tells people to this day the experience gives him chills.

He, like the parents I get messages from, was terrified. There was no logical rationale to what happened that night. And for a long time, he would only discuss the story in hushed tones. With this story in mind, now imagine you are the toddler running into your parents' room panicking over an unseen entity.

Questions to Consider

How would your parents have responded?

How would they have shared the story? Or would they have kept quiet?

What makes you believe this would have been the way they responded?

Are your memories of the stories your parents tell more like this? Were they unnerved by the paranormal?

When you imagine yourself in both stories, was it easier to envision how your caregivers would respond in one story as opposed to another? Did the positive or negative experience resonate more strongly? Take a moment to explore your story further.

Questions to Consider

Did your parents or caregivers discuss death with you?

Did your parents or caregivers believe in intuition and/or the paranormal? Do you know?

> *Do you recall a situation or occurrence that could be classified as paranormal that took place in your childhood home? How did your parents or caregivers react?*
>
> *Were there a number of these stories? Or were these stories few and far between?*
>
> *If stories were recounted, were they told with pride? Or was the story told in hushed tones?*
>
> *Can you talk to your parents or caregivers about your intuitive development today? How do they respond?*
>
> *When you think about the story/stories, how does it make you feel about intuition? Or how does the lack of a story impact you?*
>
> *Do you think the environment provided by your parents or caregivers helped your intuition? Why or why not?*

If there is acceptance and a positive regard for intuition and the paranormal, then you are in luck. Your parents imprinted a foundation that supports intuitive development similar to the supportive environment in which I was raised. If this is the case, your inner voice is probably already directing you and you will have little to overcome to embrace your intuition. If they did not, that doesn't mean the foundation they created has to work against you. Awareness of beliefs imprinted upon you is a tool of empowerment. Awareness allows you to transform your actions and beliefs from passive and reflexive, to active and deliberate choices that further your life goals to be in alignment with a belief system you define. Deliberate choices allow your soul and intuition to guide you, as opposed to the opinions placed on you by others.

Consider Rachel. Her parents are both engineers. It should come as no surprise that math and science were highly regarded in her family. Following in her parents' footsteps, she studied computer science in college. Upon graduation, she obtained a job in her field, but her heart yearned for something else. In seeking that passion, she turned to her Christian summer camp, a place where she had found joy over the years. She found happiness as a camper and the summer she served as a youth counselor she was convinced she found her calling. When she informed her mother and father she was leaving her lucrative technical job to become a youth director at a church, they were concerned. While they had instilled a love of math and science in their daughter, her passion for the church was one she came upon on her own. Their concern was elevated further when she shared that the church was located more than a thousand miles from home. Despite their opposition, she followed her heart, and while the job didn't work out, she found something more important, her spirituality and her intuition. She listens, she is guided, and the decisions she makes are right for her, no one else.

You can be like Rachel. It's not easy, but you can do it. If you find it challenging decoding the spiritual belief system imprinted upon you by your relatives, specifically your parents, don't start there. Instead, like Rachel, start with your life goals and aspirations. Reflect on what it is you want in life. If you immediately start dreaming of a baby, marriage, more money or a stellar promotion, delve deeper. These goals lack substance and won't truly bring you happiness, for in life it is not the object or status that brings you joy, rather it is how those things make you feel. Ask yourself: why do I want more money or the promotion? What is it I think I will gain from achieving these goals? Perhaps you perceive additional money as bringing you security or facilitating your ability to travel.

If you yearn for a child, perhaps it is your desire to nurture another human being or the love you assume the child will bring to your life.

While reflecting on your aspirations, begin to consider the manner in which you believe your parents or caregivers would respond to these ambitions. A question many new parents ponder is *what will my child become?* Parents often weave their own hopes and dreams into their children's lives. An example is the woman who always wanted to be the dancer and projects that onto her daughter. With good intentions, parents put their wishes on their children. My father, for example, encouraged both my brother and me to consider federal jobs. It is a place where he found security, benefits and lucrative pay. It is not a place either my brother or I would have found satisfying. Fortunately, my parents had always instilled the belief that if I work hard, I can do anything I put my mind to.

Take a moment and reflect upon what your parents wanted for you in life.

Questions to Consider

What goals and aspirations did your parents have for you? Was there a direction they encouraged over another?

Do you feel as though your parents ever lived vicariously through you?

Are your hopes and dreams the same as your parents'? Or, do they differ?

Do you feel your parents' beliefs have influenced your own goals and dreams? If yes, how so?

> *Have you taken steps to make them happy? If yes, have you sacrificed your own goals?*
>
> *How have your parents supported the development and execution of your goals?*

As you reflect on these questions, it is important to note that your perception of their response is more telling than their actions. Your perception of their desires provides insight into your own belief system. You are likely consciously or unconsciously acting in response to your assumptions of their desires more than their actual actions. Unfortunately, if you believe their hopes for you are not in alignment with your own, your intuition and the manifestation of your life purpose may be hindered as you take steps to minimize that dissonance. For example, while in college I originally elected to double major in neuroscience and psychology. This decision was motivated by my belief that my parents valued a foundation in the sciences which neuroscience provided and my passion at the time, psychology, didn't. Since then, I have come to realize the major I chose didn't matter to my parents, they just wanted me to be happy.

You very well may be like myself, making assumptions. These assumptions are based on the belief system you have adopted due to your environment. Fortunately, there are many things you can do to take steps to change these assumptions and live through intuition. The first step is awareness. As you begin to identify the ways in which your experiences are influencing you today, you come to the second step, which is remembering that you always have a choice. Their beliefs are not your beliefs. Every day you have the opportunity to write your own book. Once you realize that, your intuition will speak to you and your goals will become easier to achieve.

CHAPTER FOUR
CHILDHOOD PEERS & SIBLINGS

"Childhood friendships are a key building block for relationships in later life. They hone skills for future relationships, demonstrate the importance of emotional commitment, facilitate the separation from family, safeguard against feelings of rejection and loneliness, and ease the transition to adulthood."
Molly Countermine

It is apparent that your parents have a significant impact on your values and attitudes. That perspective, however, is only one post in the foundation that is your belief system. Psychologists such as Lev Vygotsky and JR Harris assert that while a parent's influence is pivotal, one's peer group plays an even larger role in the implementation of one's viewpoints. In his theory of internalization, Vygotsky proposes individuals observe and adopt their peers' social norms as their own belief system. In short, an individual succumbs to peer pressure. This happens as a result of an individual's problem-solving interactions within an environment.

Consider the following. The home environment as created by one's parents is relatively controlled and often habitual. Parents often strive to establish order through routine, such as dinner and bedtime; rules, like saying please and thank you; and chores that may include making the bed and washing the dishes. This order produces stability in a child's life. Additionally, in ideal situations that child feels love and approval. As a result, within the home environment a child will know the expectations of his or her parents and respond accordingly without much consideration. Unlike the home environment, interactions with peers are not as predictable. Situations are often new and complex; individuals have conflicting routines and philosophies; and peers respond with judgment as opposed to love and acceptance. As a result, the child is navigating unknown terrain and each action is carefully contemplated. For example, I ask my husband to grab my keys. Completing this task is simple, for he knows that nine times out of ten my keys are hanging on our key rack, whereas if his friend asks him to grab his or her keys at his or her house, the retrieval is more challenging. To accomplish the task, my husband first must consider where his friend may have left the keys and then find them in an environment foreign to him. Even if the friend tells my husband where they are, for example on the kitchen counter, it will still take him a greater amount of time to locate the keys due to unfamiliarity. Similar to my husband, a child in new environments with peers is confronted with making conscious choices about his or her actions. These choices, whether they occur once or through repetition, have a significant impact on an individual.

    A child's response to a situation will be dependent on two main factors: the foundation created by his or her parents and the behaviors he or she observes his or her peers exhibiting. With this information, the child will respond in one of two ways: 1) the child's actions will replicate his or her peers' actions, or 2) the child will weigh the actions of his or her peers with the belief system instilled in him or her by his or her parents.

Let's explore this concept further as we reflect upon an excursion my daughter and I took to a local playground. It was a busy day and about sixty kids were running around. Before scampering off to play, my daughter took a few moments to observe the scene and was ultimately drawn to an outdoor wooden kitchen set. The wooden kitchen was outfitted with colanders, pots, pans and ice cube trays. Three little girls were playing there when my daughter walked up, introduced herself and joined the fun. Since these little girls were pretending the wood chips were "noodles," my daughter began doing the same.

In this situation, the behavior exhibited by the little girls had little impact on my daughter's overall behavior as their behavior was in alignment with her typical behavior. My daughter loves to play in her kitchen and often helps while I'm cooking. That's not to say her peers did not shape her behaviors. Through observation, she adopted the specifics of what she was "cooking" because upon joining the girls she too was cooking "noodles," whereas at home she usually prepares cupcakes. Additionally, like the girls who were using wood chips as props, my daughter did the same, but at home she typically uses her imagination. In this instance, my daughter's peers had an effect, but it was minimal and short lived. Upon returning home, despite having wood chips in our yard around her outdoor play house, she returned to using her imagination.

An interaction that occurred later in the day demonstrated not only the impact peers have on us but also our ability to choose our response to those influences. After playing with the little girls, my daughter was drawn to the music station where a boy between the ages of six and eight was playing. In this area there was a small table about 36 inches tall that had two large pizza-sized indents. Mallets were attached to the side of the table for kids to hit the indents, which resulted in a variety of tones. The boy decided rather than play music on the apparatus it would be fun to climb on it. He pulled himself up, stood tall and started jumping. My daughter was mesmerized. Her wide eyes made it clear there was an internal struggle occurring. His actions looked fun, but her continued look back and forth between me and his mother indicated she felt his behavior was not appropriate. As she continued to observe the situation, neither his mother nor I said anything. His mother allowed him to jump. I just watched my daughter. After a few minutes, her desire to play in the same manner got the better of her. She inched towards the table and positioned herself to climb up. Before she did, she gave me one last look. Her eyes were screaming for permission. I simply shook my head "no." That's all it took. She immediately backed away and ran to play in another part of the playground. The foundation imprinted upon her by my husband and me in this situation outweighed what her peer was doing, but that is not always the case.

My husband and I have experienced my daughter's peers' influence when it comes to the restraint she exhibits in controlling her emotions. We have been fortunate for our daughter remains calm and collected in most situations. This is not to say she never has tantrums. For example, while in Disney World she had a meltdown outside *The Many Adventures of Winnie the Pooh*. To this day, I'm uncertain what triggered the tantrum, but she threw herself on the ground and wailed. With me standing over her, she laid on the ground kicking, screaming and crying. And despite the comments from parents regarding our parenting choices, we let her have the fit. I stood over her to ensure she would not be trampled and let her get the frustrated and exhausted energy out.

Outbursts like these have always been the exception rather than the rule and have occurred infrequently. Instead, we assisted her in managing her escalating emotions through hugs, breathing techniques, even encouragement to cry and release her emotions. When those techniques failed, we'd attempt to divert her attention. These tactics worked most of the time. Even at Disney in one of her worst meltdowns to date, she cried for only for a couple of minutes before she had worked through her emotions and was smiling.

This has changed upon entering school. Unlike my daughter, we discovered not all her peers are as good at managing their emotions. It's understandable, for they are preschoolers after all. Unfortunately, as my daughter has observed her peers throwing tantrums and subsequently getting their way, her behavior has regressed. After observing the child in her class who hits when frustrated, my daughter started walking over and hitting my husband. After observing her classmates crying and subsequently getting their way, my daughter started to do the same. Are these kids bad? No. Is my daughter bad? No. She has witnessed her peers' behaviors and chosen to adopt them, even though they are different than those instilled in her by my husband and me. Unfortunately for her, the behaviors she was exhibiting did not have the intended outcomes, and she is already modifying her behavior back into alignment with ours.

Social influences of peers like the three just described happen every day. Children are introduced to their peers' behaviors and belief systems at day-care, school, and the playground; in the store, doctor's offices and your own yard; through playdates with friends and family; even on television. The interaction doesn't have to be active such as when my daughter was playing with the little girls at the playground kitchen; it very well may be passive, such as when my daughter was watching the boy on the table. Every interaction and observance, however, affects the child.

The impact of the interaction can be strong. It can also be minimal. The degree the impact will have on a child is determined by the following factors: 1) the child's genetic disposition and resulting behavioral and personality traits; 2) the strength of the parental influence; 3) the frequency and duration of the interactions; and, 4) the environment within which the interaction takes place. Let's investigate this further by continuing the example of my daughter at the playground. Despite being intrigued, the boy's actions had little influence on my daughter as she ultimately opted not to mimic his behavior. The following are a few possible reasons why her behavior was not swayed: 1) my daughter has always been a people pleaser and she knew if she proceeded despite being told no, I would not have been pleased; 2) neither my husband nor I say "no" frequently and she is given a lot of freedom; as a result she knows that if she is told "no," there is good reason for it; 3) this was a single interaction with the boy, and there was no relationship; and 4) there were plenty of other kids and activities to interact with on the playground, so she wasn't limited to the one activity. As a result, the draw of the behavior became minimal and she moved on. Had factors in the equation been different (for example, had her best friend been the one jumping on the table or had my husband said no as opposed to me or had there not been a dozen other activities to occupy herself with) she may have chosen a different path.

The impact a child's peers have on them is influential because like the parental impact, the imprint occurs within the child early on and often without a conscious awareness. While the behavioral choices made are easier for an adult to observe and process, a small child who has not developed emotionally, socially or intellectually is unable to objectively make decisions based upon his or her environment and history. As a result, a child is easily swayed by peer pressure and lack of impulse control. In fact, many adults find this challenging as well! Fortunately, you don't have to worry about learning how to manage impulse control or stand up to peer pressure yet; that will be discussed later in the book. Right now, let's focus on how interactions with childhood peers have influenced you and your intuition today.

Start by reflecting on your childhood.

Questions to Consider

Do you have siblings? If so, how would you describe your relationship with them?

What are your earliest memories of childhood friendships? Did you have friendships before elementary school?

Did you choose your friends? Or were the friendships based upon your parents' friendships?

Did you find it easy to make friends in unfamiliar circumstances? Why or why not?

Did you see these friends frequently? Or were the interactions sporadic?

As you recall these relationships, what feelings are ignited?

As I reflect on my early friendships, I immediately picture DJ. He was the son of a close family friend. Born only a month before me, our mothers were pregnant together and learned to parent together. Our parents got together frequently for adult and child playdates, and when it came time to send DJ and me to preschool, they elected to send us together, which was convenient not only because we started school equipped with a friend, but because we lived in close proximity, we could carpool. Memories of those car rides fill me with pure joy. We would sing along to the radio and as we'd approach the "big" hill, we'd giggle and let out a *"Weeee!"* all the way down.

My memories of early childhood are all filled with laughter, acceptance and wonder. If yours are the same, this is supportive of your intuition and your life purpose as they create positive, safe experiences during your formative years. Happiness, security and approval are important because they provide a strong foundation of feeling loved and accepted for who you are, key ingredients in accepting your intuition and chasing your purpose.

In contrast to my experience, my husband's recollections of his early childhood friendships are filled with sorrow and loneliness. During my husband's formative years, his father had custody as his parents had divorced. He recalls spending more time with his cousins and local kids than his father. When asked to recall his childhood friends, he glumly responds that *"he didn't have many."* He remembers he and his brother would be dropped off with whomever was available to watch the boys regardless of my husband's feelings while his father would go to a bar or for a ride on his motorcycle. While I recollect my friendships with joy, my husband associates those friendships with a lack of control and abandonment. As he grew, this lack of joy from friendships continued. After his father's death, my husband's mother received custody. Shortly after, she married a man in the Navy, and she and the boys moved to wherever her husband was stationed. As a result, my husband was always the new kid attempting to fit in. This impacts him and his intuition significantly today in that instead of listening to his inner voice and chasing his goals and desires, he instead uses his energy to fit in and please others. He makes assumptions about what others want and adopts them as his own desires. As a result, he is perpetually unhappy.

His story is complicated in that not only does he try to fit in, but the feeling of lack of control plagues him as well. He could not control the babysitters his father selected or the location his stepfather would be stationed next. His life and subsequent friendships were outside his control. As a result, he continues to feel a lack of control in his life. When he does have an item he wishes to manifest, it is not uncommon for him to say, *"Dawn, this is what I want. Can you help me manifest it?"* because he doesn't believe in himself enough to do it for himself.

If you find your history is similar to my husband's, don't worry. Intuition and the manifestation of your dreams need not elude you. You can do this by identifying a friend that did support you, even if he or she was not one from your childhood. Identify a friend who was a kindred spirit. Focus on the acceptance and joy you felt with that individual. Bring memories of the time you spent with that individual to the forefront, and any memories that do not bring that same joy, dismiss.

Questions to Consider

Why did you choose the person you did?

How has this person supported you in the past?

Why has this person supported you in the past? What were his or her motivations?

> *What did/do you gain from having this individual in your life?*
>
> *Is this person currently in your life? If not, why? If so, how does he or she support you today?*
>
> *What did/does he or she gain from having you in his or her life?*
>
> *How has he or she impacted who you are today?*

Positive, supportive friendships help an individual feel invincible. When surrounded, you know you are not alone; instead, you have a team. The earlier in life you have these friendships, the more likely you are to listen to your intuition and chase your dreams. Unfortunately, not all friendships will be supportive. Some "friends" will wish to control you. Some "friends" will chastise you for being different. I was blessed that it wasn't until the fourth or fifth grade when I was between the age of nine and eleven that I first felt unique and chastened for it. This aligns with developmental psychologist Erik Erikson's theory that between the ages of six and eleven a child begins to recognize the differences between his or her abilities and the abilities of other children. A child will learn where his or her abilities excel and where he or she lacks skill. This stage overlaps with the next stage of development during which Erikson proposes a child begins developing his or her own unique identity. The development of a unique identity begins between the ages of twelve and eighteen, and it is during this time frame that an individual will struggle with those personality traits that set him or her apart. Some will find comfort in standing out and begin down the path towards their life purpose; others will seek to conform to a role defined for them by society, be it by their parents, peers, educators or community. It is during these years that the innocence children begins to dissipate as they become young adults who apply the scientific method and logic to their everyday lives.

It was during this developmental evolution that I realized for the first time my experiences and beliefs were different. I was staying overnight at my friend Collette's house. Collette lived in the neighborhood and due to our proximity, at least once a week one of us would cart our sleeping bag over to the other's house. We were giggly girls and often spent the night playing dress up or board games like Mall Madness, watching movies such as *Grease* or going gaga over the New Kids on the Block. This night was different. My friend's birthday was approaching. Her father decided to mark this milestone by introducing us to horror movies. My family has never been a fan of scary movies, so the scariest movie I'd seen at that point was the *Wizard of Oz*. Being a sensitive kid, even *Annie* made me cry as I worried about her climbing up the tower as she tried to get away from her would-be captors. However, not wanting to be a wimp, I didn't say anything as he put on *Night of the Living Dead (1968)*.

For those of you not familiar with the movie, as the name of the movie suggests, it is a zombie film. As with all zombie flicks, the dead come to life and are driven by their desire to eat fresh brains as the protagonists fight to escape and save their own lives. Filmed in the late 60s, it is a horror movie produced well before special effects, so as an adult I see the hokeyness. As a child, I did not.

Within twenty minutes of the movie starting, I went from being timid to bawling. My friend's poor father surely felt guilt, and more than that, he had no idea how to comfort the inconsolable child in front of him. At first, he teased and pretended to be a zombie himself. I'm sure it was his way of trying to get me to laugh. He then gently reminded me it was a movie and that zombies aren't real.

What he didn't know is that I held a belief that people never really die. As a result, it logically made sense that their bodies could be reanimated. If reanimated, why wouldn't they would want to eat brains? Vampires drank blood after all.

Once the movie was turned off, I did eventually calm down. That night I didn't sleep. I kept the blanket over my head and watched the door and the windows, afraid a zombie would break in at any moment. For weeks after watching the movie, I slept with the light on or on my parents' bedroom floor. And for months I was hesitant to stay over at friends' houses, convinced my house was safer.

Eventually that fear dissipated. After that night, I was grateful neither my friend nor her father said anything about the movie, but at the same time, I was ashamed and embarrassed. Years later, I know it had an impact on me. I still don't care for horror films. Nor do I like sleeping near a door. I recently learned it also had an impact on Collette. How do I know? I was honored to officiate her marriage. As we were preparing for her nuptials, she asked if I remembered the fateful night. During our conversations she admitted she too had been spooked by the movie, but she never understood why it had elicited such a dramatic response from me. She said she had always known the fear stemmed from some place deep within me, touching a cord she didn't understand until now. She imparted that seeing the career path I have taken, she now understands my fear much better. With hindsight, we both have come to peace with the circumstance and have grown because of it. It made me realize I was different and that I had to be careful about how I presented myself. Through the subsequent conversations with my friend, it has made me realize I have also become comfortable in that skin.

Let's reflect on your life.

> ### Questions to Consider
>
> *Was there a time in your childhood when your peers made you feel different or unaccepted? Specifically reflect on the ages of six to eleven.*
>
> *Was there a time you forced yourself to be brave in front of friends despite being scared?*
>
> *When you consider the times you were different, are you still different? Or did you adapt your behavior to be in alignment with your friends?*
>
> *How do these reflections make you feel today? Do you feel closure? Or does discomfort remain?*

The growth from difficult situations is significant. Unfortunately, there are times we don't get closure or peace with situations that occur, and as a result they continue to haunt us and limit our growth. An event that haunts me to this day is one in which my peers weren't as gentle as my friend and her father. This next story also takes place at a slumber party where five or six girls were staying at a friend's home. It was the spring of my fifth-grade year. We were old enough that we didn't play with Barbies anymore, but many still brought our special stuffed animal or blanket to the sleepover. We giggled about the boys we liked, had fondue, did each other's hair, nails and make-up, watched movies and for the first time told spooky stories. Amongst them was the story of "*Bloody Mary.*" If you are not familiar with the tale, the story goes that if you stand in front of a mirror with the lights off and say her name three times she is supposed to appear in the mirror. My friends were intrigued, and they eagerly wanted to see if we would be able to summon her.

The thought of trying to summon a ghost terrified me. I wasn't an experienced medium at the time; in fact, I don't even think I knew what the term "medium" meant. What I did know from everything my grandfather had taught was that summoning a ghost was not a good idea. I pleaded with the girls not to go through with it. I presented them with all the reasons why it was a bad idea. As I continued to talk, I remember the moment my friends realized I wasn't joking but dead serious and truly frightened. They looked at me as though I were foolish and absurd. As they laughed at me with contempt, it was only then I realized they didn't believe conjuring a ghost was real.

Filled with disbelief and beguilement, I wondered, *"How could they not believe in ghosts? Why was this such a preposterous idea?"* I didn't understand what was ridiculous about this. At that point, I had seen spirit and was consciously aware that ghosts were all around us.

That night I had a lot of time to sit and ponder these questions because in my shock my friends locked me in a darkened basement. Outside the basement door they teased me and chanted for ghosts to appear. Unlike the day I was introduced to horror films, I didn't cry. Instead, I sat silently and prayed that any spirit that appeared would go away, just as my grandfather had taught me. I also prayed for guidance. Needless to say, I kept my mouth shut the rest of that slumber party.

This situation had a significant impact on me, and it still does. I was immature enough not to have the skill set to process what had happened, but I was old enough that I didn't want to go to my parents and have them fight my battle for me. As a result, I distanced myself from everyone who could have helped. I don't recall telling my parents about it. I didn't talk to my friends about ghosts again because I didn't want a recurrence of the situation. This was the moment I began to shut out my intuition, and more specifically, ghosts.

Most kids have this moment. I was a little older than most as this moment usually occurs between the ages of seven and nine. Children move from seeing imaginary friends and being sensitive to no longer seeing spirit and being more deliberate in the expression of their feelings. It is also at this point when children begin to not be surprised by disappointment.

Reflect on your life, specifically between the ages of seven and nine.

Questions to Consider

Do you remember having imaginary friends, seeing spirit or auras, or feeling energy when you were little? If so, when did that stop?

When would you say you "grew up"?

When was the first time your innocence was shattered?

Do you recall a time when you felt as though you had to be brave, even though you were terrified?

Was there a situation that made you realize your belief system wasn't in alignment with that of your friends? How did it make you feel? How did you respond? Did you shut up? Or did you adapt?

Was there a time when your friends' actions hurt you to the core? Why did it hurt?

As you reflect on these situations, it is important to recognize that it is not what happened to you, but rather, how you look back on that situation now and how you allow that circumstance to define you. For example, the

Bloody Mary debacle was painful. As the little girl, I was confused, felt foolish and rejected by my friends. Upon reflection, I am inspired by that little girl. I asserted my beliefs. I stuck to my guns, even though it put me in a situation that was uncomfortable. And despite realizing that my beliefs were not in alignment with my peers and my friends thinking I was silly at best, I might have kept my mouth shut, but I never dismissed those beliefs. I did not let my peers' opinions define me.

That does not mean the situation did and does not still cause me pain and discomfort. To this day, especially with new friends, I tread lightly and feel individuals out before discussing my chosen career. Additionally, I am "friends" with some of the girls who tormented me that night due to social media. Upon viewing images of the children they are raising, my first thought is, *"God help those children,"* followed by, *"And if their kids are anything like them, help their friends."* These thoughts demonstrate no matter how far we have come, we always have more work to do.

Take a moment to reflect on the impact your peers have had on your development.

Questions to Consider

When you and a peer(s) disagree, do you stand up for what you believe in? Or do you remain quiet?

Have you allowed others to define you? Or have you marched to the beat of your own drum?

Do you show your friends your true self? Or do you hide that from them?

Do past experiences with friends impact your present actions?

As you reflect on your history, you may recall traumatic defining moments such as the Bloody Mary incident. But you may also recollect seemingly insignificant interactions that stick with you, despite their outwardly petty nature. Do not dismiss these memories as they speak volumes. While not an example from my childhood, consider the following. A friend introduced me to his significant other recently and after only a brief conversation, the significant other flippantly commented that I was *"obviously a Hufflepuff."* This reference to *Harry Potter* infuriated me as I questioned *"Why Hufflepuff?"* As with most *Harry Potter* aficionados, I have pondered what House I would be sorted into if I were to attend Hogwarts and have always been felt an affinity towards Ravenclaw. His choice of Hufflepuff was in discord with my perception of self and triggered the frustration. Just as quick as that frustration hit, it dissipated. How? I realized it didn't matter what he thought of me; the only thing that matter is what I believe about myself. In that there is strength.

Explore the recollections that outwardly appear to be petty. There is a reason you are unable to shake the feeling. The reason is likely as demonstrated above: an individual is categorizing you in a manner that is in disagreement with your identity. Finding resolution is powerful, especially in light of the fact that individuals make assumptions about others every day, and you have faced and will face situations like the one just described throughout your life, time and time again. Because of that, if you don't believe you responded with that strength in the past, you don't need to beat yourself up, for you will have plenty of opportunities to define yourself in the future. In fact, by exploring your intuition you already are! And chances are you are already standing up for your beliefs without even realizing it. For example, I may have thought I was keeping my mouth shut regarding my spiritual beliefs, but in hindsight it was leaking out left and right. My favorite books were those in the *Goosebumps* series. My favorite television shows were those with witches, from *Bewitched* to *Charmed*. In middle school, I did a report for English on spirit guides and meditation; in high school health class I did a project on dream interpretation and dragged my friends to the hypnotist that performed at the county fair; and in college, not only did I learn all the campus ghost stories, I also chose to live in the haunted dorm. I surrounded myself with experiences that fostered my belief that there was something more than I could see with my naked eye. Thus, consciously and unconsciously, I started choosing friends who supported my experiences and accepted me for whomever I chose to be.

Before we move on, feel free to go back and reflect on the questions again. The more you consider your history, the more you are reminded of who you are. The journey into your past not only assists you in identifying where you came from, but it will shine light on who you are today. And from big decisions to little ones, you will have a greater understanding of your actions and from this moment on be able to make more deliberate choices. You have the choice every day to choose how the experiences you have had influence you.

CHAPTER FIVE
ADULT PEERS

"I'm not in this world to live up to your expectations and you're not in this world to live up to mine."
Bruce Lee

Intuitive children face ridicule from their peers. While we would hope kids grow out of that childishness, unfortunately, one need only look to the media to see that is often not the case. In fact, the gossip proliferated by adults is often more damaging and hurtful than that spread by children.

Considering this from a psychological perspective, it makes sense. Until an individual reaches late adolescence, he or she does not have the ability to fully comprehend and project the consequences of his or her actions. As a result, children have little comprehension of the long-term psychological effect their actions have on their peers. Think back to the example of my friends teasing and locking me in the basement. At the time, they thought it was funny. Once they released me from the basement, they included me without hesitation, behaving as if nothing had happened because to them it hadn't. They had no realization how damaging their behavior was.

The same is not true of adults. Adults have years of experience and most understand that their actions have potential for both short and long-term ramifications. Unfortunately, adults also have the option to disregard these consequences. As a result, some adults act in a vindictive manner with the intent of hurting another to further their own interests. These individuals purposefully use information to hurt others. They identify weaknesses and/or uniqueness in another and use it to manipulate, control or belittle their target. Unfortunately, because there is a stigma associated with intuition, specifically psychics and the paranormal, it is not surprising that some individuals identify and exploit this trait. As a result, some fear their own intuition and beliefs because they fear they will be judged by others. You may be one of these individuals. You may fear that your friends will laugh at or ostracize you, like my childhood peers did. You may fear your spouse will think you foolish. You may also fear your beliefs will worsen an already shaky relationship with your in-laws. Some even fear that if their employer discovers their beliefs, their reputation will be tarnished, or worse, they will lose their job. The perceived consequences of one's intuition and beliefs can be crippling. It's no wonder an individual, perhaps even you, would be hesitant in sharing your beliefs and willing to conform to society's norm.

I understand. In some cases, the perceived consequence is the reality. I have participated in psychic fairs where picketers have shown up to rally against the event. They have stood outside the venue carrying signs, spitting on patrons and in one instance defacing a vendor's vehicle. I have received correspondence from organizations and individuals quoting scripture, informing me I have sold my soul to the Devil and encouraging me to repent my sins. These situations were scary, and I feared for my personal safety, but these judgmental individuals had little impact on my beliefs or subsequent lifestyle choices. I do not know the picketers or the individuals writing me letters, and as a result, I have no personal investment in their opinions. Additionally, my parents created a strong foundation and instilled confidence in my beliefs. That confidence shines through the shadow cast by others.

Today I am not shy about my belief system. That has not always been the case. Coming out of the proverbial closet as a medium was hard. I never feared my relatives' response to my ability, for as you know, they had always nurtured and cultivated it. I was hesitant about sharing my abilities with friends, acquaintances and colleagues because I feared they would respond as the picketers and letter writers had. For years, I chose to fly under the radar to avoid difficult and uncomfortable interactions. I've been successful in some situations, failed miserably in others. The same may be true for you. Even while trying to avoid uncomfortable conversations and situations, you may still experience both ridicule and judgment from employers, relatives, friends and strangers. I have, even when I thought I prepared myself.

How do I prepare? Aware my beliefs and the nature of my business could conflict with another's belief system, in both social and professional situations, I am always transparent. I know there are individuals who do not believe it is possible to communicate with deceased loved ones or intuit the future, and that even if individuals believe it is possible, they may not see it as being in alignment with God's will. By being open and honest, not only about my beliefs but who I am, I give potential employers and friends the opportunity to opt out of the relationship, which I'm okay with. I don't want to hide part of myself. Nor do I want to convert another to my way of thinking. We all have our own truths to live by. As a result, with emerging new relationships I cautiously share that I am a small-business owner offering spiritual guidance to my clients. My experience has been if someone's beliefs are in conflict with mine, they ask no more questions. On the other hand, those whose beliefs are in alignment with mine or who are undecided, will ask for more details, at which point I divulge that I am a medium.

Being candid has served me well most of the time. I have attracted friends who appreciate and are respectful of my work. And in my professional relationships, I was respected by both my peers and my superiors. Those who were interested in my personal business asked questions. For those who weren't, our relationship remained professional, and I found I was not judged for my beliefs but respected for my work and work ethic.

I wish I could say this happened one hundred percent of the time, but I don't live in a Utopia. Like many of you, I have had encounters that made me question my policy of transparency, the most potent being in a job that made me reevaluate my entire life. There were signs of trouble from the beginning. While interviewing for the position, Andrea, my would-be boss, made it clear she was skeptical of my spiritual beliefs. Despite that, she hired me for the position. I assumed we would both shelve our opinions and silently agree not to discuss the subject. I wasn't hired because I am a medium, I was hired because I was a talented grant writer.

Avoiding a spiritual dialogue and focusing on the work at hand worked well until a random Thursday afternoon about three months after I started. At about 3:00pm, Andrea came barreling into my office to request that I stay late. She informed me there was a meeting at 6:30pm that she needed me to attend. I regretfully informed her I would not be able to accommodate her request. The meeting was outside of business hours, so given the short notice I didn't think this would be a problem. This powerful woman was not accustomed to being told no, so my response caused her to become quite belligerent. Unwilling to accept my response, she attempted to bully me into attending the meeting, and when I informed her it wasn't possible as I had prior obligations, she insisted on knowing the nature of those commitments and why they were more important than my job. In hindsight, I should have ended the conversation by simply stating it didn't matter the nature of those engagements; I was unavailable. Instead, I informed her I had clients scheduled and believed it would be unprofessional to reschedule them with such short notice. I made sure she knew I had no problem attending any meeting she requested, even outside of business hours, as long as I had ample notice that would give me the opportunity to appropriately arrange my calendar. Rather than responding to my request, Andrea stormed off muttering a number of expletives. I left the matter knowing that a discussion would get me nowhere.

A couple of weeks later, I found myself wishing I had taken the time to have a heart-felt dialogue with Andrea regarding the incident. We were meeting with partner organizations, many of whom I was meeting for the first time, to discuss our collaborative efforts in a community initiative. I don't recall what initiated Andrea's comment, but during the meeting she made a sarcastic remark about how I "believed" I could talk to the dead and that maybe I should go "do a dance" to get the "fates to align" to accomplish the seemingly impossible goals being assessed.

In that moment, a wave of emotion flooded through me. It was apparent my boss meant to belittle and diminish me in the eyes of our partners. I was embarrassed and wanted to cry. I was angry and contemplated quitting on the spot. I was disappointed that this is how Andrea, a woman I had respected, chose to view me. Then something unexpected happened. The last person in the room I expected to respond positively to the comment spoke up. She asked, *"Do you work in Lily Dale? I've always been fascinated by that place."* With that, the palpable tension in the air dissipated and my belief system became a non-issue, at least in the eyes of these community partners.

The interaction, however, made it clear my belief system was and would be an issue for Andrea. More importantly, I knew that even if she were able to resolve her internal conflict over my values, my feelings regarding her behavior would not be resolved. She judged me not on the merit of my work, but rather on her perceptions of my faith. Worse, she attempted to use that information to belittle me. Had this been an isolated occurrence, I may have been able to forgive it. It wasn't. This behavior was Andrea's nature. Throughout the few months I had worked for the organization, I witnessed her identifying attributes in each of her employees that she could, and did, exploit. It was her way. You've likely experienced an individual who does the same thing. What have you done in that situation? I chose not to subject myself to that treatment any longer. Less than a year after accepting the job, I left. She asked me to stay on for a month to complete a project. I didn't. Only loose ends remained on the assignment, so I left in two weeks. Her request was an attempt to get her way one last time.

Leaving this position was scary. At the time, I had irons in the fire, but another job had not been secured. Fortunately, I had my business to fall back on. It would take nurturing, for I had devoted long hours to the position and had neglected my work and clients. The uncertainty was better for my soul than being stifled and judged. Quitting the job was a hard leap, one that I recognize not everyone is able to make. But I had to.

Unfortunately, the prejudice I was subjected to is not unique. You will encounter miserable, demeaning people like Andrea. If you give those individuals a chance, they will work towards destroying your confidence and steering you away from your life purpose. Their snide comments and actions both underhanded and blatant, will cause you to question yourself and your worth. It's important to recognize you do not deserve that behavior, and every day you have a choice in how you choose to respond. You can be reactive, responding quickly and without much thought or consideration. For example, I could have walked out of the meeting the day my boss belittled me and not turned back. You may respond proactively and deliberately, as I did. I reviewed the situation objectively, weighed my options, created and executed a plan that would minimize the discomfort. You may procrastinate, as a colleague who worked under that same manager did. Andrea brought my colleague to tears multiple times a week. Finally, after three years of being degraded, she left. Ultimately, it doesn't matter how quickly or slowly you respond: what is important is that you find the strength to empower yourself to stand up for your values and yourself.

Let's take a moment to reflect on your life.

Questions to Consider

Have you encountered a situation in your personal or professional life where you have been demeaned and diminished simply based upon your beliefs?

If so, what tactics were used to control or change you? Were his or her methods outwardly aggressive? Or were they more passive in nature?

> *Did the assaults to you and your belief system occur from the onset, or did they occur gradually over time?*
>
> *Which fears of yours did he or she uncover and exploit?*
>
> *How did you respond to the aggression? Did you ignore it or did you stand up for yourself?*
>
> *Did the individual's opinion affect the way you view yourself? Have you changed because of it?*
>
> *How did it make you feel? How do you feel about it today? Did this situation affect future situations?*

Reflecting on these incidents and uncovering your feelings regarding them is important because times when we are presented with conflict and criticism are opportunities for reevaluation, reinforcement and growth of our beliefs. While in the moment I was hurt and the furthest thing from grateful, in hindsight I am thankful for my experience with Andrea. While her comments were not constructive in nature, I used them to reevaluate my goals and values. It caused me to evaluate my motivations for taking the job in the first place. When I had accepted the position, friends were disappointed because they reckoned I should have focused on my business. I opted for the position because I feared the lack of security of being a small business owner and liked the thought of a steady paycheck. Once in the uncomfortable environment, I realized the confinement and judgment were more debilitating and chose to step out of fear and focus on what was truly important to me.

You have the ability to do the same thing, but it's not easy. Others will express their opinion. They may even try to control you with it. Their view may or may not be in alignment with your own. But another's belief does not define you. Ultimately, another's impression only defines you when you let it. Unlike a child who is a passive recipient of philosophies and experiences where beliefs are imprinted upon him or her without conscious knowledge and/or choice, adults can consciously respond to their circumstances and choose whether they agree with others' opinions.

Again, not allowing another's opinion to define you, being objective and most importantly, following your intuition, isn't easy. It wasn't easy quitting my job without another lined up and my business in the lowest place it had been in years while being the primary provider. It wasn't easy sorting out my feelings and determining what was the smartest move while I received mixed messages from my friends who were supportive and my family that was conflicted. It wasn't easy not knowing what the future would hold and knowing my husband and I would need to work hard and be financially responsible. We needed to sacrifice. Despite this, I followed my heart, and the next year I had the most successful year. Like me, you may find it hard to follow your heart, but trusting your gut is always the right thing to do.

Empowering yourself and dismissing others' opinions is hard. Fortunately, there are tactics you can employ that will assist you in empowering yourself towards manifesting your desires. The most important tactic is to learn to say no. Every day we take on tasks and responsibilities that are not in alignment with our goals. How often do you agree to assist a friend or cause even when you don't have time? Do you speak up when you don't agree with a statement a friend has said, or do you leave it? How often do you allow someone else to define you because you aren't up for the fight? In these instances, you are letting someone else define who you are. Your friends, relatives, teachers, colleagues and even strangers will try to influence you. They might even use tactics that make you question yourself and some are really good at it. But you are better. You have a strength. You have a purpose. And the universe will help you achieve that, that is, if you embrace your strengths and live your life with character and purpose. This requires you to say no when requests are not in alignment with your values and your purpose.

Consider the following example. Kristen is a colleague whom multiple mutual acquaintances have encouraged I forge a business relationship. She is a sweet woman and from our conversations I gathered we have similar philosophies, which reinforced the belief that a professional relationship would be advantageous to both of us. Everything was going smoothly until we tried to arrange our calendars to meet and solidify the collaboration. We'd go back and forth and back and forth trying to arrange our calendars. When we'd finally set a date, time and time again something would come up which would cause the need to reschedule, or worse, I'd show up and she wouldn't. When this would happen, I questioned her intentions and questioned myself: *Was I not good enough? Had I offended her?* After six months of this, I recognized that perhaps the universe was trying to tell me the relationship wasn't as beneficial as I believed it to be and that I needed to say no. Instead of putting energy toward this business relationship, I decided to focus on other projects that upon reflection are more in alignment with my goals. As a result, I experience less stress and am happier. When you focus on your goals, you'll find that same happiness.

With this example in mind, let's take a moment to reflect on your life.

> ## Questions to Consider
>
> *Is there a time you spent trying to force a relationship, personal or professional? If so, how did it end? How do you feel about it today?*
>
> *Is there a situation in your life today that you are trying to force? Why?*
>
> *What in your life would bring you happiness?*
>
> *What situations support this happiness? What situations hinder it?*

Answering these questions will begin to bring insight, and taking action will bring you joy. That doesn't mean you will experience instant gratification. Many of your hopes and dreams will take time, perhaps even a lifetime, to manifest. However, if you listen to your intuition and live purposefully, joy will be manifested. How can I be certain? Every spirit I have ever encountered remarks on the benevolence and loving nature of God, the universe, Allah, Creator, whatever you choose to call the omniscient force surrounding us. That energy wants you to be happy and to achieve your desires. That being said, what you want is not always what you need. Your intuition will direct you towards and manifest what you need and your life purpose, not necessarily what you want. As a result, what is manifested may appear different from what you envisioned.

The universe also works through your intuition to assist you in manifesting your goals and life purpose because you are a unique individual destined to leave your mark on the world in your own special way. You are filled with exceptional talents and only you can share those abilities with the world. Because of this, it is important that you don't allow others' opinions to direct your actions. It is also why it is so important that you don't allow where you came from or all the beliefs that have simply been imprinted on you define who it is you are and what it is you are doing. That is not you. It is simply the environment that has created you.

It's also important that while you look to others for inspiration that you do not try to become someone else. This is something I have struggled with. Upon hitting a limbo in my life, I had been advised to emulate an individual I admire and not only model his or her business, but model him or her as an individual. At first, I tried. It was awkward, hard and I failed miserably. Why? I'm not them. I'm me. You need to be you too. That's not to say we cannot look to individuals as inspiration, but each of us needs to honor who we are as individuals. How do you do this? You stop being a passive participant by continuing to ask yourself questions. Look within yourself and find not what others tell you you're good at, but what lights a fire within you. In fact, what others perceive you to be best at may not be what brings you to life or what you are meant to do.

For example, I was always good at math and science. Perhaps this is because I was a daughter of a nurse and an accountant. Perhaps, I am genetically predisposed. Or maybe the environment created by my parents supported these skills. Despite having a knack for math and science, from a young age I loved writing. As a little girl, I would spend hours writing poetry and short stories. I am grateful my family was supportive. My parents would read the stories and offer critique. My aunt even submitted one to a magazine to validate me. Yet at school I was told my writing was only so-so. While I excelled in math and science, in English, my marks were average. As a result, I worked hard to be better. Unfortunately, the hard work didn't pay off, and I was devastated when I wasn't selected to be part of AP English. That decision caused me to believe no matter how hard I worked, I was never going to be good enough. As a result, I abandoned my dreams of writing and instead focused my energy on the sciences, a subject in which I knew I could excel.

Despite abandoning the dream, the passion for writing never waned. Instead, I found ways to express it, and I was excited when a former superior and mentor took notice. She felt I had a knack for writing and simplifying complex concepts. With her support, the organization trained me to become the in-house grant writer. I loved what I was doing. And the outcomes, the grants my submissions secured, demonstrated that I was succeeding. In merging the sciences and writing, I felt I had found my calling.

That confidence was lost in an instant upon taking the position under the horrid executive, Andrea. Remember her? Shortly after the debacle with our community partners, she informed me that she was disappointed in my performance since my writing was mediocre at best. She demanded that every report and document be reviewed by her. To demonstrate my inadequacy, she'd take a red pen and critique reports making changes, mostly stylistic. Her actions were condescending and each page was marked up top to bottom. Each time I received the marked report, I felt like the high schooler and doubted my abilities. That doubt caused me to check and recheck the accuracy and language. A process that used to take two or three reviews turned into dozens. This reinforced her statement that I wasn't good enough.

But as you know, I chose to walk away from that toxic environment. How did I come to the solution that it was healthiest for me to leave? How can you determine what will truly make you happy? First think about your hopes and dreams. What are they? Are you looking for the love of your life? Or a new position? If so, ask yourself why? What is it that you want from the love of your life? What is it that you want from a new position? Take my desire to be an author and to write. I don't want to be an author just to be an author. I want to write because I want to normalize mediumship and, more broadly, intuition. I have a message I want to spread and that not only makes me happy, I would be disheartened if I didn't follow that passion. Reflecting on your own passions, what would disappoint you if you did accomplish in your life? What goals are within your power to complete? Once you have that in mind, you can start thinking about the way you are going to get there.

Once you become committed to your goals and start taking steps towards achieving them, you may be surprised that your peers start to change as well. You are rubbing off on them. When an individual is living his or her truth, he or she is empowered. That confidence is attractive to others and it is hard for people to be judgmental. Since proverbially coming out of the closet, I have witnessed this to be true.

When people learn that I am medium, I typically receive positive or neutral responses. This even occurs in situations where I experience apprehension over sharing my belief system. This was the case when my husband and I enrolled my daughter in nursery school. To say I felt trepidation about sharing my profession with other parents is putting it mildly. I didn't have apprehension because I was concerned about other parents' perception of my husband or me, as we were not looking for an opportunity to socialize with other parents by joining a parents' group. We enrolled our daughter in preschool because we observed her desire and need to socialize with her peers. She yearned for friends and community, not us. But the parents' and teachers' influence on our daughter's would-be-classmates concerned me. As discussed in a previous chapter, parents' opinions have an impact on their kids. Preschoolers are especially impressionable. With this in mind, the mama bear in me imagined the worst-case scenario. What if a parent had a visceral response like my boss or the protesters? What if he or she expresses his or her disgust to his or her child? His or her judgement of me could then potentially affect his or her child's perception of my daughter and how she may be treated by her peers in class. If that interaction turned negative, what would be the long-term impact? Rationally, I know that she, at some point in her life, is going to have negative interactions with her peers. I'd like that to be when she is more emotionally and psychologically developed and can better process the situation. And selfishly, I don't want to be the cause for that negative interaction. I want to be the safe place she can run to as we work through it.

Due to the fear, on the application I responded "self-employed" for mother's profession. At the parent orientation and in small-talk with other parents, I avoided conversations that would lead to the question: *"what do you do?"* Fortunately, the question rarely came up.

Yet I could only dodge the bullet for so long. I was outed one morning while my husband was conversing with the school's Parent Board Chair. This is not uncommon as our daughter attended a cooperative nursery school, and each family is required to volunteer time to assist school operations. Our family's participation hours were completed by my husband when he volunteered to be the school's webmaster. As webmaster, he and the Board Chair met frequently while the school prepared to launch a new, user-friendly website. Despite seeing him frequently, she rarely saw me, which was abnormal since mothers and grandmothers are present more than fathers, and she asked me the dreaded question, *"What do you do?"*

As you know, transparency is my motto, so I simply responded, *"I am a medium."* And just like that the cat was out of the bag. I could feel myself release a big sigh of relief as a weight was lifted off my shoulders. I was even more relieved when I saw a huge smile cross her face. Two days later she chased me down to tell me she had texted a bunch of the moms and they were wondering if I would do a gallery event for the school.

I look back and laugh at the angst I caused myself. You probably cause yourself that same amount of angst from worry and/or fear. You need not! I have found that how adults respond to you has a lot to do with how you perceive yourself and approach them. If you demonstrate a lack of confidence, people won't take you seriously, which will negatively impact your intuition. My husband experiences this frequently. He is Mr. Mom and due to my work schedule, he ends up being the one to take my daughter to the playground, school or to other public places to socialize. While she is playing, he finds himself in conversation with the parents of the other kids. He has commented that on several occasions as soon as the topic of what I do comes up, the conversation abruptly stops and the parent he was just conversing with packs his or her kid up to leave. He has also noticed that if he sees these parents again, they avoid him like the plague.

I have never had that experience. Or if it has occurred, I haven't noticed it. Instead, I often can't get people off the topic of spirituality and intuition. I find that upon meeting someone new, all the questions that have been building inside regarding spirituality come out. This may be because for the first time he or she has someone whom he or she perceives to be an expert on the topic to answer these questions. If this is the case, it makes me sad. In the few minutes I end up talking with the individual, I see them walking away standing taller and having hope. It may also be because I am confident in my beliefs.

At this point in my life, I have developed a thick skin and don't allow others' opinions to impact me. In fact, I often find myself being the individual with opinions that impact others. I encourage you to do the same. Embrace your beliefs and know you will not be able to win over everyone. Then again, the only one important for you to win over is yourself. If you do nothing else in this life, learn to do that.

CHAPTER SIX
INSTITUTIONS

"Human social institutions can effect the course of human evolution. Just as climate, food supply, predators, and other natural forces of selection have molded our nature, so too can our culture."
Peter Singer

Individuals you interact with are not the only factors that influence your perspective. Institutions you are affiliated with, be it fraternal or social organizations, your work place, church or school, also influence your perspective and inner voice.

Institutions, much like individuals, carry an energy and ideology. This ideology is declared through an organization's mission, vision and value statements. All formalized organizations from businesses and fraternities to churches and schools have these statements. These philosophical tenets drive an organization's work. Take for example, Facebook's mission statement is *"To bring the world closer together."* As you read this, it is evident that the media platform throughout its evolution has consistently worked to create a community and bring people together, no matter the physical distance. Now consider Twitter's mission, *"To give everyone the power to create and share ideas and information instantly, without barriers."* At first glance, these two statements may appear very similar. Both promote the sharing of information. On further examination, it is apparent that subtle language differences exist. Facebook states it wishes to *"bring the world closer together,"* whereas Twitter states it wishes to *"share ideas and information"*; nothing in the Twitter statement talks about bringing individuals together – rather, the emphasis is placed on the information or data being shared. These subtle differences are powerful representations of the execution of these modalities. Facebook is flooded with posts regarding the lives of your "friends," whereas Twitter is flooded with "news" and commentary. If you prefer one platform over another, it is likely due to the execution and content created, and that preference likely happened without you having any insight of the creator's goals. It is in this way institutions have an impact on you. As a result, having insight into an organization's ideology will bring you insight into not only the influence it may have on you but also why you were attracted to it to begin with.

Let's start by exploring fraternal organizations. Fraternal organizations are social institutions from fraternities and sororities, to the VFW and the American Legion, to the Rotary or Red Hat Society. Organizations such as these experienced greater popularity in the 50s, 60s and 70s, yet many still exist today and are thriving. Participation in these organizations starts at all ages of life. For example, a child may become a Girl or Boy Scout, a college student may join a fraternity or sorority, and an adult may become a Freemason or Eastern Star member. These organizations are important in understanding your inner voice and the manifestation of your goals in that they provide you with a support system and an avenue to express your passions and purpose. If you are or have been a member of one of these organizations, they likely have had or are having a significant impact upon you.

To explore this concept, take for example that I am a member of the Alpha Delta Pi sorority. I joined my sophomore year of college and while I wish I could say I was inspired by its motto *"We Live for Each Other"* or by its values of friendship, truth and sincerity, I joined because many of my friends were already members. And while those values may not have motivated me at the time, they have stuck with me, and the lessons I learned during my time in the sorority impacted me greatly. In college, it was my sorority sisters who were there in my greatest times of need. The same can be said today as my best friend is a sorority sister. Additionally, the philanthropical spirit of Alpha Delta Pi was instilled in me during my college years. Alpha Delta Pi supports the Ronald McDonald House and to this day, this cause has a special place in my heart.

The influence of institutions is minimal when compared to the individuals in your life, yet the impact still exists. Reflect on groups you are/have been affiliated.

Questions to Consider

What organizations are/have you been affiliated with? Why did you join or become affiliated?

How did these organizations impact you?

What are the mission/vision statements of these organizations?

Do these mission/vision statements define who you are? Are they in alignment with your life goals?

As you consider these organizations, always keep in mind they impact your decisions today, however minimal.

CHAPTER SEVEN
SCHOOL

"Education is what survives when what has been learned is forgotten."
BF Skinner

Fraternal organizations often have a minimal impact on your identity. This is primarily because you have consciously chosen to be affiliated with the organization likely because the social institution is in alignment with your attitudes and beliefs. For example, you are unlikely to become affiliated with the NRA if you are staunchly opposed to guns and support gun control. If those are your attitudes, you are more likely to join or affiliate yourself with Everytown for Gun Safety. You will consciously choose the social organizations you affiliate with because they further your beliefs. The same cannot be said of academic institutions, especially those your attended during childhood. Rather, the academic institutions you attended as a child were chosen for you deliberately or inadvertently by your caregivers. For example, my husband and I took pain-staking care in selecting my daughter's preschool. She, however, had no choice in the matter. These institutions, however, have significant impact on one's identity and inner voice.

Academic institutions an individual is enrolled, such as the preschool, elementary, middle and high school, college or vocational institution, influence his or her perceptions and belief systems significantly, for not only does he or she spend the majority of his or her formative years attending these institutions, but these institutions are responsible for his or her education. The instruction garnered from these institutions goes beyond reading, writing and arithmetic. Perhaps more importantly, educators encourage their students to think critically about and experience the world.

The strategies utilized to impart knowledge to students vary by institution. Some schools applaud rote learning or memorization and place a focus on results. These institutions are less concerned about the student application of concepts but instead focus on the demonstration of knowledge through tests. By contrast, other institutions stress and foster exploration and creativity with the belief that while it may take the child longer to learn, the child will ultimately retain the information and have the ability to apply the concepts in new environments. For example, a classroom that honors rote learning may be forced to memorize and recite the Gettysburg Address. Students in a class that fosters exploration may pick apart Lincoln's famous speech line by line dissecting the content for its meaning but may not be required to commit to memory the words. Similarly, instead of having students recite addition and multiplication tables, the child, through demonstration, will be shown that one plus one equals two. Both learning styles are effective and have their place in a learning environment. What is important is not what method was utilized, but rather, the awareness of the learning style you were educated with as a child will be the method you employ to learn new concepts today. For example, my husband attended schools where memorization was preferred. To this day, for him to grasp a new subject he finds himself needing to repeat the information to himself numerous times. I, on the other-hand, attended schools that focused on experiential learning. As a result, if I am learning a new skill, until I see it put in practice I struggle with comprehension. Understanding this informs how you approach situations in life, and more importantly, the manner your intuition communicates with you.

Academic institutions vary not only in the educational models they employ, but also in the lessons they teach. Throughout the world, objective subjects such as reading, writing and arithmetic are taught in a relatively universal manner. Educators at an elementary school in New York City, Berlin, Hong Kong and Boise, ID will all teach their students that one plus one equals two, even if it means using the words one plus one or uno y uno.

While the curricula in these subjects may be universal, the same cannot be said of history, literature and even science. Depending on the culture in which you live, the lessons delivered may vary. For example, there are publicly funded schools in the United States that teach creationism as opposed to Darwin's Theory of Evolution. Additionally, it is safe to say that the history lessons regarding the Civil Rights Movement of the 60s will be different in a white, suburban classroom outside of Boston and an inner city, predominantly black classroom in Chicago and different again for students in a rural community in Mississippi. The teachings will vary for a variety of reasons, including the students' experience, the background of the educator and the culture of the community. For example, the students in the predominantly white, suburban classroom may never have experienced racism, whereas racism may continue to be a very real experience for those students in the predominantly black, inner city classroom. As a result, the children from the white, suburban classroom may view the Civil Rights Movement as history, believing inequities have been overcome and equality has been achieved. A student from the inner city, black school may know that not to be true based on his or her experience. Similarly, an educator's background and experience will influence the presentation of that material. In many cases, the educator's background will match the experience of his or her students. For example, an individual who lived through the Civil Rights Movement will present the information in a different manner than an individual born and raised long after the movement. Not only that, a white educator is likely to present the information differently than a black. Unfortunately, since individuals are attracted to institutions that are similar to those in which they are raised, it is more likely an individual that attended a suburban school will teach in a suburban district and an educator reared in the inner city will teach at a city school. With limited diversity, this proliferates bias. The culture of the community also proliferates bias. The schools in Boston and Chicago with a history in industry will have a very different viewpoint from the school in rural Mississippi with a history of slavery. Experiences are different, and as a result, students are presented with a different perception of the "truth."

You as a student are taught to perceive the world in terms of these "truths." These truths become a foundation from which you approach situations in your life. Continuing the Civil Rights Movement example, there may be a universal message that to overcome social injustice people must act and resist injustice. Your background and the educational system you are raised within will determine what the manner of action is. For some that will mean participating in marches and protests, for others that may mean raising money for a cause, and for others still it may mean elevating the situation to violence.

When I reflect on my educational background, I consider myself blessed. I was raised in an upper middle-class town with one of the best public-school systems not only in the area but the state. The school system was rich with opportunities, and I took advantage of many of them. The district had a program called Spectrum designed for gifted children. I participated in the class in elementary school and through it was introduced to critical thinking activities such as logic puzzles, books such as *The Phantom Tollbooth* and *A Wrinkle in Time* and was encouraged students to think outside the box. I also participated in Odyssey of the Mind (OM), a competition where a team of seven kids are given a problem and encouraged to solve it creatively. Through this program, my team went back in time to Pompeii, journeyed with the Old Man in Hemingway's classic, made robots and beautiful music. Throughout my education, I was continuously encouraged to imagine the possibilities. This, like my family's belief system, facilitated my intuition as it inspired me not to be limited by what I see with my eyes, but rather journey as far as my imagination would take me.

I know I was blessed because this experience was drastically different from my husband's. As mentioned earlier, my husband's stepfather was a career seaman. With his stepfather in the Navy, he attended schools all over the country and throughout the world. This afforded him the ability to experience different cultures, but the educational systems he attended were limiting. Unlike the programs I participated in where I was given a blank piece of paper and urged to create, he was given a problem and a series of solutions. His creativity and imagination were curtailed, even when he ventured to explore them. As a result, his intuition was stifled as well.

Let's take a moment to reflect on the academic institutions you attended.

> ### Questions to Consider
>
> *In the educational system you were enrolled, was a focus placed on repetitive learning and test scores or were you encouraged to think outside the box?*
>
> *Did you feel comfortable and supported in school?*
>
> *When you had an idea, was it celebrated or was it dismissed?*
>
> *Did you feel like you succeeded in school?*
>
> *When you failed, were you encouraged to get back up again?*
>
> *What did your educational system prepare you for in life?*
>
> *What were the greatest lessons you learned from your educational system?*

Being celebrated and positively reinforced are significant factors related to one's educational growth. The support one receives is not only via the system, but perhaps more importantly via the educators within it. A talented, reassuring and compassionate educator affects a child's life significantly. Unfortunately, the same can be said of a demeaning, callous and rigid instructor.

Throughout school, I was blessed with a number of kindhearted teachers. For example, my first grade teacher, Ms. Munro, was a saint. It was the first year I was attending a full day of classes and struggled because I easily became bored. I would complete the work before my classmates and would sit around waiting. Waiting until the ants in my pants got the better of me, that is.

Anxious, I'd stand up, walk out of the classroom and wander the halls. This was obviously unacceptable, and as a result I spent a lot of time in the principal's office. Despite the improperness of my behavior, I don't recall the principal or Ms Munro ever scolding me or telling me I was a "bad" kid. Instead, I felt love and support from the two of them. To find a solution, they thought outside of the box. A computer was brought into the classroom, which back in the mid-80s was unheard of. When I, or other students, completed our work we were instructed that we could play reading and math games while we awaited the next activity. With a task to preoccupy me, I never again walked out of the classroom.

Throughout my formative years, I had many teachers like Ms. Munro. In fact, the prevalence of these teachers outweighed the educators that were unsupportive or judgmental. Their support has transcended school. I have had several teachers whom I remain in contact with to this day. Unfortunately, my husband cannot say the same. Perhaps this is due to his not being in one school for a long duration of time as a result of his stepfather's career, but from how my husband as spoke about the educational systems, he did not perceive them as fostering these relationships. Take a moment to consider your educators.

Questions to Consider

Did you feel nurtured by your teachers?

Did you have a teacher who was supportive of your development positively or negatively? If so, how?

How does that educator's teachings still resonate with you today? How has their words assisted in the development of your inner dialogue?

The educational system you experienced as a child continues into adulthood as it also impacts the selections you make regarding higher education and career. In some districts, the measure of success is the graduation rate. For other districts, the measure of success is not only graduation rate but also admittance to top tier schools. As a student, you will be influenced by the district's objectives. For example, if a district is concerned over its graduation rate, more effort is going to be placed on the child who is struggling than the student who without any effort is obtaining As. In this situation, if you are the student achieving high marks, you may have little support from the school and may be on your own when it comes to figuring out higher education. On the other hand, if a district's focus is on admittance to top tier schools, the focus will be on the high achieving children, which in turn will also pull the struggling children up. In this situation, whether the student is high achieving or not, the student assistance will be given to help the student achieve his or her maximum potential.

This difference was demonstrated by my husband's and my educational systems. Having attended military schools growing up, it should come as no surprise upon graduation he opted to attend the Virginia Military Institute in Lexington, VA. Following an injury, he attended ITT Tech in Syracuse, NY. Both programs focus on preparing the student for a specific job; at VMI to participate in the military, at ITT to be a Network Systems Administrator. This aligned with the type of system he was raised in. In fact, he struggled after the injury at VMI when he initially enrolled at a liberal arts college. Not prepared for that type of education, he struggled. Conversely, I attended Allegheny College in Meadville, PA. It is a small liberal arts school. When considering colleges, Allegheny was attractive because it required each student to complete a senior thesis prior to graduation. The senior comp, similar to a graduate program thesis, is completely designed and executed by the student. As more than 30% of students continue on to some form of graduate education, this project prepares them for such.

Again, it is important to note neither is better than the other; it's just a different mindset that has been taught. These different mindsets have impacted us and are apparent in the manner we think through and approach tasks today. For example, my husband and I approach house renovations in completely different ways, and my office is a fantastic example. One of the selling points of our home was that it had a back porch where I could do readings. The space wasn't ideal, and over the years we made modifications to make it work. A modification that became a necessity after my daughter was born was the removal of a window between my daughter's bedroom and the office as she would peek in during readings which I deemed distracting at best and unprofessional at worst. When we discussed the project, my husband was focused on what it would take to complete that one, single task. I, on the other-hand, envisioned the entire room undertaking a transformation. New walls, windows, ceilings suddenly floated into my mind and what was to be a simple fix, became a big project. He couldn't imagine my vision at the onset since his focus was one the window. After lengthy discussions, he agrees that undertaking the larger project was the smart move because had we not, the wall that would have been created where the window had been would have been taken out to run electric to the room in the future.

Being able to envision the transformation was my intuition at work and is largely a result of the educational environment in which I was raised. When thinking about the room, I thought outside the box and deliberated on more than just the project at hand. Considering limitless possibilities supports intuition because you are not limited to what you see in front of you, but what could be. This supports the idea that there are still discoveries out there to be made and we are the explorers. The spiritual realm is just one more place to explore, and I have fun exploring it every day. We chart our own journey. No one does that for you. I had amazing teachers who continued to push me and my peers outside of the box. I know my husband can't say the same.

Fortunately, it's never too late to keep learning and developing and to create a new blueprint. All you have to do is keep your mind open. One of the ways you can do this is by exploring your spirituality and intuition through lifelong learning. As I mentioned in previous chapters, I have taken classes in mediumship development and reflexology, but that is not the only education that has promoted my intuition. Being part of a leadership development network, attending book clubs and lecture series all have inspired me to think in a variety of different ways. You can do the same thing. Around each corner you will find new teachers, new lessons, new ways of thinking, each of which will bring you closer to understanding yourself, hearing your intuition and manifesting your heart's desires.

CHAPTER EIGHT
THE WORKPLACE

"Your work is going to fill a large part of your life, and the only way to be truly satisfied is to do what you believe is great work. And the only way to do great work is to love what you do. If you haven't found it yet, keep looking. Don't settle. As with all matters of the heart, you'll know when you find it."
Steve Jobs

Children spend the majority of their waking hours in school. This is another reason an academic institution has a significant impact on an individual's perspective. Similarly, an adult spends the majority of waking hours at the workplace. Thus, it is reasonable to conceive that the organization that employs you has an impact on you and your perspectives. This is true of the corporation that employs you today, as well as businesses you worked for five years ago. Their institutional culture will influence you. This is applicable even if you are self-employed and the architect of your own work environment.

The workplace affects you as a result of a variety of factors. For one, the workplace will likely bring you into contact with a diverse group of individuals. As discussed previously, peers have an influence on your mindset. At work, whether self-employed, a contractor or a staff employee, you may interact with a team of colleagues, superiors or subordinates, even clients. Some of those interactions may be brief and leave little lasting impression. Other individuals may have a significant impact due to the long duration of time spent together. Colleagues' personalities and dispositions will also influence the strength of the effect. A peer that is mild mannered will influence you less than one who is loud and obstinate. Additionally, a colleague is more likely to influence your perspective if his or her opinion directly impacts you as opposed to if it doesn't. Let's consider a few examples. When I worked with Andrea, my husband found me to be short-tempered and generally unhappy. This occurred whether I was in the office for a few minutes or more than ten hours. Due to her overbearing personality, her mood would rub off on me. On days she opted to diminish a subordinate other than myself, my disposition was better, whereas the days she elected to put me in the doghouse, I was short-tempered, lacked confidence and was dissatisfied. Not all examples are bad. Consider my interactions with Stacie. She is a level-headed, compassionate executive level employee. After being hired for my first "real" job, I found myself working under her on several projects. She mentored and guided, and while she offered criticism, it was always constructive. Unlike with Andrea, where I found myself cranky, I was energized by this work. More than that, I found myself modeling Stacey's behaviors. Take a moment to reflect on your experiences.

Questions to Consider

Is there a current or previous boss that made you feel nurtured? If so, why? What traits did they possess?

> *How would you categorize the relationships within your work environment? Why?*
>
> *How does your work environment impact you?*
>
> *Does a past work environment influence you today?*

In addition to individuals, the overall culture of the organization will have an impact on your perspective and resulting intuition. The organization by which you are or were employed has a mission, vision and core values. These statements direct the organization both externally and internally. The manner in which the organization operates will in turn have an impact on you. Let's explore this concept further. Prior to operating my business full-time, I worked with the P2 (Pursuing Perfection) Collaborative of Western New York. I was employed by this organization for a little more than six years, and I would classify it as the most enjoyable job, outside of my own business. The individuals I worked with were dedicated and passionate. I had a supportive and generous boss. Additionally, the organization challenged me intellectually and facilitated personal and professional growth. While no job is perfect, this was as good as it gets. I feel blessed to have been part of this institution.

While my colleagues at P2 impacted me significantly, so did the culture of the organization. To explore this further, first consider P2's mission: *Create a healthier Western New York*. The dedication to create a healthier community was not only demonstrated by the projects the organization undertook within the community but also within the organization's internal operations. For example, the executive director insisted healthy food options be available at every meeting and physical activity was promoted.

A philosophy of healthy living was demonstrated not only by the organization, but also through the lifestyle of its employees. Several members of the staff, including myself, became members of Community Supported Agriculture (CSA) programs. Through these programs we supported local farmers and gained access to healthy foods. Staff members participated in 5Ks and half marathons together. The year half the staff became pregnant, as P2 promoted breast-feeding initiatives, most of the new mothers chose to nurse their infants. The healthy lifestyle philosophies transcended the workplace into the employees' actions outside of work.

You could argue that individuals were attracted to P2 because of its mission. You could contend that because of their predispositions, these employees, had they worked for another organization, would have partaken in the same healthy lifestyles. You may be correct. The organization did not create a healthy lifestyle perspective in its employees. The individuals who participated in the 5Ks and half marathons were runners when they joined the organization. While I didn't participate in a CSA prior to working at the organization, the majority of my produce shopping was at farmers' markets when the weather permitted. The impact the institution had was that it further supported the beliefs through peers and education. By furthering those beliefs, the beliefs have become more deeply ingrained.

Let's take a moment to consider an organization you worked for.

Questions to Consider

What is the mission statement of the organization? If you aren't sure, look it up.

> *In what ways was this mission executed within the work place?*
>
> *What attracted you to the organization?*
>
> *How does the organization's mission align with your own belief system?*
>
> *Have you changed since working there? If yes, how?*

As you reflected on the organization you worked for, did you feel the institution had a significant effect on you? You may not have. Some organizations will have more impact on you than others. The following factors will determine the degree to which the organization will influence you. The first factor to consider is how closely aligned your goals and belief systems are with the organization's. For example, I was attracted to P2 because of the mission of the organization. Due to my own healthcare struggles, I knew firsthand the challenges an individual could face while navigating the healthcare system and was passionate to improve that. The goals of the organization aligned with my own; as a result I was personally invested. Conversely, when I think back to my first job at a movie theater, I had less of a personal investment. While I liked going to the movies, I was never passionate about it. In fact, I have always been just as content to rent a movie and watch it at home as go to the theater. As a result, the culture of the organization had a much smaller impact on me. You will find this to be true for you. If the goals of the organization are not aligned with your unique goals, interests and beliefs, the organization will have a minimal impact on your perspective and resulting actions.

Another factor that influences the degree to which the organization will impact you is whether or not you feel valued by the organization. If you feel valued or as if you are part of the team, you are more likely to be influenced by the organization. For example, P2 was a small organization. As a result, all employees had a voice at the table. Having the ability to weigh in on the operations of the organization reinforced its beliefs and in turn my beliefs. A great example of this is the organization's breast-feeding initiatives. At the table was a woman who was extremely passionate about breast-feeding as she felt it was the earliest intervention towards healthy lifestyles. As a result, whenever a grant surfaced, she lobbied to have breast-feeding worked into it. Unfortunately, there were many times my knowledge of the grantor led me to believe a nursing initiative was not in alignment with the funding opportunity. However, coming to that agreement together made me supportive of breastfeeding. This is evidenced in that when my daughter was born, I didn't even consider not nursing. On the other hand, while I vividly recall and am passionate about my work at P2, when I reflect on the initiatives at the organization led by Andrea, I was ambivalent at best, cynical at worst. At that non-profit, I knew there was only one voice that mattered, Andrea's. As a result, the goals never became my own. Again, take a moment to reflect on your own experiences.

Another factor that influences the impact the organization will have on your perspective is the length of time you've worked for the institution. It goes without saying that the longer you have been employed by an organization, the bigger the impact it will have on you. For example, take Courtney and Virginia. These two women are teachers in the same school district. This is Courtney's first year and having put in thirty years, this is potentially Virginia's last. Being new to the district, Courtney is vibrant and full of new ideas. Virginia, on the other hand, knows the district is limited and is less likely to offer new suggestions falling back instead on the district precedence.

Finally, the level of enjoyment you garner from the organization will affect its impact on you. The more enjoyment you get from the organization, the greater impact. For example, P2 was not only in alignment with my personal goals, it was also a fun place to work. Colleagues would routinely go out for lunch and dinner together; one of the major funders hosted bi-annual conferences and P2 sent a number of representatives to attend (I was blessed to attend conferences in both Denver and Washington, DC) and, perhaps most importantly, we laughed a lot. Have you had a job like this? Take a moment to reflect on the impact it has had.

For all the reasons mentioned above, it is important you are selective about the organization you are employed by as it will impact and solidify your preexisting beliefs. It reinforces the message you tell yourself every day. That being said, take a moment to reflect on the following idea. My generation, and perhaps yours, was raised to believe we should find a career that we love and, moreover, we should love going to work every day. I believe this concept has brought millions of individuals unhappiness and discontent. Why? Because many have misconstrued this statement to mean that one's career is his or her life purpose. I don't believe this is the case. Like many generations of individuals that have come before, one's job should not be one's purpose, but rather one's means to get there. I'm not saying an individual should hate what he or she does, but rather that it shouldn't be how an individual defines him or herself. Nor should the institution one works for define him or her. If you find the organization you work for is directing your identity and not the other way around, it is time to reconsider that organization.

CHAPTER NINE
RELIGION

"I believe firmly in the efficacy of religion, in its powerful influence on a person's whole life. It helps immeasurably to meet the storms and stress of life and keep you attuned to the Divine inspiration. Without inspiration, we would perish."
Walt Disney

Academic institutions are influential because they teach you how to think, and the workplace is notable because it is where you spend the majority of your time. Religious organizations also have a significant impact and they are influential because they provide moral and spiritual principles that may become the basis of your belief system. Faith is one of the greatest influencing factors impacting one's intuition since your faith defines the unseen forces that connect individuals. One's faith offers an explanation to life's biggest question, *"Why am I here?"* It doesn't matter if a person believes in a God or many gods or if an individual doesn't believe in God at all, each belief system provides an answer to that question, or rather, begins to. Intuition is another tool that assists you in answering that question, and better yet, once you begin to answer that question you have the opportunity to work in alignment with the universe to manifest that purpose.

The creation of your spiritual belief system likely began in the impressionable time that is your early childhood. Many parents elect to indoctrinate their children in their faith. The brick and mortar walls of the parent's religious institution, be it a church, temple, or mosque, is often the first formalized organization where a child is introduced and often becomes a place where a child feels safe and accepted. That feeling of belonging is important and supports the adoption of the beliefs, values and sometimes rules communicated within that edifice. Even if you didn't have a formalized religious background, your parents' religious or spiritual opinions impacted you.

Let's discuss the principles transmitted by religious institutions. The basic tenets of most religions are universal and include virtues such as love and respect. For example, regardless of religion, children are taught the "Golden Rule," which is stated almost verbatim in both the Bible as recorded by Luke 6:31 *"Do to others as you would have them do to you"* and the Mahabharata, a sacred Hindu text, *"This is the sum of duty; do naught onto other what you would not have them do unto you."* Similarly, despite karma being associated with Hinduism, individuals of most religions are taught their actions have consequences. In Christianity, this is seen in 2 Corinthians 9:6, *"Remember this: Whoever sows sparingly will also reap sparingly, and whoever sows generously will also reap generously."* Similarly, in the Islamic Qur'an it is stated in Chapter 17 Verse 7, *"If you work righteousness, you work righteousness for yourselves; and if you commit evil, you do so against yourselves."* These universal principles are often reinforced by the teachings and actions of one's parents, adult figures, peers and so on, for they are the "rules" by which we live and thrive. As an individual, no matter how young, sees the "truth" in these statements, he or she holds on to them more tightly. Consider, if an individual sees a benefit to treating others as he or she would like to be treated, he or she is more likely to behave in that manner. A simple example is my daughter. It is not uncommon behavior if she wants a treat like chocolate to approach me or my husband and offer us the item she desires, the chocolate. After our response, she will then ask if she can have one too.

The beliefs introduced by one's religious institution are not only reinforced within the community, but they are also reinforced through ritual. Ritual initiates a sense of belonging. For example, children typically between the ages of seven and thirteen in the Catholic faith celebrate their first Holy Communion. While the child likely does not have a choice as to whether or not he or she participates in the rite, it is at this point the child becomes an active participant. To complete the rite, the child will offer penance and for the first time receive the wafer, a symbol of the Lord, during communion. It is likely the child will not fully comprehend the spiritual significance of this ritual. The child is likely, however, to become more committed to the church through this ritual as it is steeped in positive reinforcement. The child is told he or she is mature enough to participate in a church ritual not appropriate before; a ceremony and often party are held specifically for him of her, and it is not uncommon for children to receive gifts. What child wouldn't want that? All of these positive occurrences reinforce one's faith in the institution and the adoption of its belief system. Similar traditions are held in most faiths. This reinforces the sense of belonging.

Despite being indoctrinated into a religion before one has conscious choice, religion is not bad. Parents introduce their children to religion because they themselves reaped a benefit from it. Faith is rewarding and healthy for an individual. Research conducted has demonstrated that individuals who consider themselves spiritual and/or religious are both mentally and physically healthier. And, faith creates a foundation for one's intuitive development. That being said, one's individual experience with his or her brick and mortar church may cause internal conflict with regard to his or her intuition. This conflict is most commonly expressed by those with a Roman Catholic background as individuals with this foundation worry whether developing their intuition or seeing a medium is against God's will and the Bible.

I was not raised Catholic, as a result I cannot speak from personal experience on the matter. My review of the Bible and review of Biblical scholars' work regarding the Bible, however have led me to believe that intuition is not ungodly. Rather, my experience and review of Biblical texts lead me to believe it is a naturally occurring ability bestowed upon individuals by God. 1 Corinthians 12: 7-11 states:

> *"To each is given the manifestation of Spirit for the common good. For to one is given through the Spirit the utterance of wisdom, to another the utterance of knowledge according to the same Spirit, to another faith by the same Spirit, to another gifts of healing by the one Spirit, to another the working of miracles, to another prophecy, to another the ability to distinguish spirits, to another various kinds of tongues; to another the interpretation of tongues. All these are empowered by one and the same Spirit, who apportions to each one individually as he wills.*

If you are a Roman Catholic, you may or may not agree with me, which is understandable since the Church, the interpreter of God's will, seems to be split on the matter. The *Catechism of the Catholic Church* does explicitly forbid consulting mediums, but a letter, *Iuvenescit Ecclesia*, released by the Vatican in May 2016 urges the Bishops to embrace parishioners with "charismatic" gifts, such as the gift of healing and prophecy. Conflicting interpretations and one's own uneasiness can cause further conflict. Ultimately, an individual must do one's own soul searching to find one's own answer.

That soul searching will be influenced by one's experience with a formal church. For example, Peter attended a parochial school run by nuns in the 50s and early 60s. The nuns did not allow the children to speak out of turn or think for themselves. If the nuns did not approve of Peter's behavior, he would be paddled. To this day, his interpretation of the church's teachings is black and white. Conversely, Kevin's experience with the church caused him to view its teachings as guideposts rather than hard-set rules. In the mid-90s, he and Stephanie had a child out of wedlock. The priest at his church chose to delay the child's baptism and encouraged the couple to wed. Another priest in the same church chose to baptize the child, stating, *"The child should not be held accountable for the sins of the parents."* Due to his experience, he witnessed firsthand the difference in interpretation of God's law by Holy men. If their interpretation can vary, so could his. Like Peter and Kevin, your experience will dictate how your religious and spiritual experience will impact you and your intuition.

My experience with religion as a child was unique. My mom was raised Protestant. My dad was raised Catholic. He joined my mother's church, the United Church of Christ, when they wed. We attended church regularly until I was in third or fourth grade. After that, we rarely attended.

Overall, I would say the influence of the Church was minimal. My brother and I were baptized, but, not being Catholic, we didn't celebrate communion like many of my classmates and paternal cousins. We stopped going to church well before the age we would have been confirmed, so neither my brother nor I experienced that rite. During lent, while my cousins and friends would practice sacrifice by giving up chocolate or potato chips and forgo red meat on Fridays, my family didn't partake in these traditions. We were introduced to the stories of Adam and Eve, Cain and Abel, and King Solomon. As these stories were taught, we were made aware that they weren't historically accurate and instead were parables designed as a framework to guide us to a Godly life. We were also encouraged to interpret the stories and make our own decisions around them.

Despite not having formalized religious training as a child, we weren't heathens. Instead of religion, my parents instilled virtues of morality and spirituality. They preached character and encouraged kindness, gratitude and service. They also encouraged my brother and me to converse with God as he was always listening and only he could and would provide answers to my prayers.

While I lack formalized religion, I am grateful for the spiritual lessons I learned. I believe these lessons assisted my personal development because at no point did I feel as though my beliefs in the paranormal conflicted with teachings of the Church, which is a fear many seekers express. Additionally, the spiritual lessons of kindness, gratitude, humility and patience instilled in me by my parents are virtues that assist an individual in grounding and centering. Grounding and centering are skills that are vital in the development of one's intuition.

At this time, I encourage you to reflect on your religious and spiritual upbringing.

Questions to Consider

Were you raised within a religion? If so, what?

> *What are the religion's primary teachings? Do you embrace those ideologies and tenets today? Why or why not?*
>
> *Are you still affiliated with that religion? Why or why not?*
>
> *If you are not affiliated with that religion, are you affiliated with a different one? If so, what? Why did you choose to change?*
>
> *Were your parents religious? Did they demonstrate the teachings as a child?*
>
> *How would you say your religious background helped or hindered who you are today?*

As you reflect, it's important to recognize that the "rules" placed upon an individual's lifestyle choices due to religion are more important than the application of them. For example, kashrut or Jewish dietary laws that outline a kosher diet while found in the Torah more likely have a more secular than spiritual purpose. While the source of these laws is unknown, scholars hypothesize these tenets were put in place for two reasons: 1) hygiene, as the process through which animals were slaughtered and processed ensured food was less likely to be contaminated; and 2) cultural segregation, for in a cultural melting pot an individual from a particular culture would be able to recognize another of the same culture through the foods they eat. These laws were a method by which the religion governed its people and kept them safe. Reflecting on your religious background and identifying these is important as it will give you a different view of your beliefs. You may choose to keep these traditions, but your understanding of them may be very different.

As you explore the faith-based institution(s) you have been affiliated with throughout your life, I also encourage you to study other faiths as well. This was a valuable step in my spiritual journey. Drawn to a variety of religions, I've read about Buddhism, which I learned is more of a practice than a religion in an attempt to understand enlightenment and become more zen. To understand the natural order of the world, I've read books on Wicca and Native American traditions. Not only have I read about various spiritual systems, I've participated in ceremonies to get a taste of the experience. For example, I've attended various churches and sweat lodges, participated in spiral dances and festivals. These experiences have reinforced that the teachings of most religions are universal and boil down to love and respect. If you are struggling with your religious foundation, you are encouraged to attend a gathering of a different faith. You'll be surprised how much you gain from it.

CHAPTER TEN
THE COMMUNITY

"We all do better when we work together. Our differences do matter, but our common humanity matters more."
Bill Clinton

Thus far we have discussed the individuals and institutions you are affiliated with. These factors are components of the macrocosm that is your community. Communities that influence you are large entities such as the nation and state within which you live, or small divisions such as a neighborhood or municipality. Likely it is a combination of all the above. The community, just like an institution such as a church, workplace or school, has philosophical and ideological tenets that create a culture, and so do the physical locations you inhabit throughout your life.

Variations in culture because of one's locale manifest themselves in a variety of ways. It could be from the food you eat, your dialect, to lifestyle choices and perspectives. For example, being raised in the northeast, I always had pumpkin and apple pie on Thanksgiving. My husband, on the other hand, was raised in the south and feasted on sweet potato and pecan pies. I say *"you guys,"* my friends from Pittsburgh said *"yinz"* and my in-laws in Mississippi say *"y'all."* Similarly, while I prepare each winter for blizzards by making sure my pantry is stocked and the de-ice coils on the roof are functioning, my brother-in-law prepares for tornados by practicing tornado drills and maintaining a safe room, and my father prepares for hurricane season by securing objects and ensuring the generator is working. We adapt to our environments and adopt preferences. For example, my husband will routinely request that in lieu of pumpkin pie I bake a sweet potato one. The recipes are very similar, but the flavor of the sweet potato is preferred by my husband over the pumpkin as it is what he grew up with.

While the examples mentioned above are in and of themselves inconsequential, the examples serve as a demonstration that the community contributes to your preferences. This is true of my husband's preference for sweet potato pie. It is also true in my preference for blizzards over tornados. When we receive snow, my brother-in-law is baffled and expresses to my husband that *"he doesn't know how we put up with the snow."* Conversely, when I see my sister-in-law comment on tornado warnings in Mississippi I feel the same about them as he does about snow. Where I comment, *"at least it's just snow,"* they comment, *"at least it doesn't happen often."* These preferences run deep and do impact your belief system.

For example, I was raised in a middle-class suburb. As an adult, I am aware there were times my family struggled, but as a child I was never concerned whether there was going to be food on the table or not. Our pantry and freezer were always stocked. Similarly, while I may not always have had the luxury of wearing designer clothes, my parents kept me well dressed. I also knew if I was willing to wait for a sale, my parent's would be able to purchase me the brand name clothing my wealthier friends were donning. My husband's experience was quite different. He knows firsthand what it is like to worry about having food on the table. When he was ten on the first Thanksgiving after his father's death when his mother obtained custody, his mother informed the boys that in order to have a nice meal she was going to bounce a check. Additionally, once my husband entered high school, because money was tight he was expected to pay his own way. He purchased his own clothes, his own vehicle, a computer. Our different backgrounds affect the way we perceive life today. My husband has developed an expensive taste. Having the ability to afford foods he couldn't when he was younger, he routinely orders the most expensive item on the menu even when it's not a food he typically enjoys. I, on the other hand, will not. Because of my experience, I do not deem "what I can afford" as a measure of success but instead focus on the pleasure it brings.

Similar to the factors discussed earlier in the book, the impact the culture of your community has on your belief system may be hard to recognize. This is especially true if you are living in the same community where you were born and raised and/or have not travelled extensively. Even if you have moved or travelled extensively, you may still not realize the impact the community has on your perspectives. Not having moved beyond the region where I was born, I consistently remind myself that life is different elsewhere. Fortunately, I have been afforded the opportunity to travel extensively both by my parents as a child and through career opportunities.

If your view hasn't been extended much beyond your home, tools exist that provide insight into your community that you may overlook by being immersed in it. The tools were generated by marketing firms after recognizing the significance of community values. These organizations conducted an immense amount of research to determine characteristics of communities. The research categorizes areas not just in terms of broad cities and states, but the data has been drilled down to the zip code level. This information collected by ERSI in the Tapestry Segmentation Project is available online to anyone wishing to know more.

Curious about this data in relation to my upbringing, I examined the data. I revealed that the communities I've lived in consisted of college educated individuals with more liberal ideologies. The individuals living in these areas often support the arts and like to travel. As a result, it is no wonder that my intuitive gifts have been at the minimum tolerated, and in most situations accepted. When my husband and I moved into our home, I was a little concerned how we would be perceived, especially since some of my business would be conducted from my home office. When we moved in, however, I found that we were embraced fully. My neighbors next door were the first to discover my profession when they noticed I had rocks scattered throughout the yard. They were intrigued. When the neighbor across the street discovered my line of work, she shared that she had an aunt that was a medium. No one in the community batted an eye.

I was also curious about my husband's upbringing. As mentioned earlier he was the stepson of a career Navy seaman and as a result moved quite a bit. A common thread amongst the places he called home was that they were hard workers either scraping or just getting by. The data reveals these individuals do not use credit cards and prefer to pay their bills in person. In addition, they are more likely to have small town and old-fashioned values. It comes as no surprise that his family, while accepting of our lifestyle, are more uncomfortable with it. It also provides insight into my husband's own dissonance regarding his beliefs.

Take a moment to reflect on your community and the philosophical ideologies you were raised with.

> ## Questions to Consider
>
> *Were the views within your community more conservative or liberal?*
>
> *Were the views within the community radical or extremist? Or did they have more moderate leanings?*
>
> *Was there a great deal of diversity?*
>
> *Was conformity encouraged? Or, were open dialogues and conversations encouraged?*
>
> *Did you travel and experience different cultures? If so, what did you learn from your experiences?*

As you ponder your experiences and your community, know that the more diversity you experience and the more open the community you live within, the more adaptable you become and the greater ability you have to think outside the box. As a result, you will be more intuitive.

How does this happen? Intuition is simply being observant to your environment and then acting upon those observations. Throughout this book we have discussed the manner by which individuals respond to their environments, consciously and unconsciously. You may have discovered individuals are likely to conform as the do not want to stand out from the crowd or offend anyone. For example, it is not uncommon for an individual to eat a food he or she does not care for in order to not offend the host or hostess. I did this the first time I met my stepmother. She invited my father and me over for dinner and served eggplant parmesan. I hate eggplant. Despite that, I ate some so as not to offend her.

As individuals interact with different cultures and traditions, similarly they will adopt some of those behaviors. Think of this in terms of a church service. While participating in a service, you will stand when everyone else does, kneel when indicated and return to sitting when asked to. Why? Because it is respectful of the church's tradition and ritual.

The same thing goes with ideologies. After experiencing and adapting to these ideologies, an individual may have incorporated the belief into his or her own belief system. As a result, an individual who has traveled extensively or experienced a great deal of diversity is more likely to be intuitive than one who is not. That intuition has become a part of survival.

You might be thinking, I struggle with change and foreign environments. This is okay. Due to individuals' histories and dispositions, not everyone is as adaptable. Consider Mike and Michelle. This couple does not like variation; rather, they embrace routine. The couple gets up every morning at 6am. They have oatmeal for breakfast, every morning. *Jeopardy* is turned on every night at 7:30pm. Mike and Michelle stick to this routine, even after they retired. Surprisingly, they do also enjoy travelling, but they will only travel to a few select locations. Disney World is one of them. While on their Disney vacation, they again stick to a routine. They always stay at the same resort and eat meals at the same chain restaurants. While at Disney, they always go on the same rides and attend the same shows. They do not enjoy variety.

You may be like Mike and Michelle. You may not be. Take a moment to think about your life.

> ### Questions to Consider
>
> *Have you experienced a great deal of variety in your life?*
>
> *Do you find you enjoy trying new things?*
>
> *If you do, do you find you enjoy the variety? Or do you prefer to fall back on the familiar?*

Whether you prefer variety or familiarity, what is more important is that you are willing to try. If your community does not support diversity and new experiences, you may find it harder to listen to your inner voice and manifest your desires as you are encouraged to conform to the societal norm. Fortunately, if you don't fit in the societal norm that is your community, you can always choose a new community as there is likely to be one nearby that is in alignment with your beliefs.

CHAPTER ELEVEN
CHOICE

"Sometimes it's the smallest decisions that can change your life forever."
Keri Russell

A common thread among the factors that affect your story explored thus far is that your personal preference was not taken into account. Instead, you were placed in environments where you were influenced simply by being there and of which you had no control. For example, a child born into an impoverished family will experience poverty as a child. A child from an impoverished family doesn't have the ability to choose his or her parents or where he or she was born. Additionally, a child has no avenue by which he or she could change his or her circumstances. The child can't go get a job or even win the lottery. Rather, the experience is one the child survives through and develops a belief system around.

Fortunately, while an individual can't choose what factors impact him or her, an individual can choose how he or she allows the bearing those facets have in the future. That requires awareness. Developing an appreciation of the influence and acting upon it is hard, and as a result, many are ignorant. Consider Dustin. Throughout Dustin's entire life, he has been told by his family he was a disappointment. When he received an A, he was asked why it wasn't an A+. As he'd nervously get ready for a date, his mother would tell him not to bother it wasn't going to change the fact that he wasn't a "pretty boy." And, after taking the football field his father and friends would heckle him from the stands. The lack of support has had a significant influence on him today. Presently, Dustin is a marketing consultant. He has a thriving business and due to throughput issues, he often turns away clients. Despite his success, he becomes depressed every time a prospective client elects not to retain his services. He laments, *"Why doesn't anything I put effort into work out?"* and then becomes angry as he attempts to justify his value. With a focus on the contracts he didn't obtain as opposed to those he did, he feels like a failure and disappointment. Can you relate to Dustin? If not, perhaps you are like Donna. She, like Dustin, had a less than supportive upbringing. Her mother, who was often on a diet, would comment on Donna's weight. The message that Donna was chunky and could benefit from losing a few pounds was reinforced by the theater teacher who upon giving the lead to another student commented that Donna didn't "look" the part. Rather than being discouraged, Donna adopted a can-do attitude and studied nutrition. She is currently a self-employed nutritionist who coaches individuals to achieve their optimum health. She does not allow her past to define who she is today.

Take a moment to reflect on Dustin and Donna's stories; who do you believe you are more like? Why? Chances are, you exhibit characteristics of both Dustin and Donna. That is okay. It's even okay if you choose to be like Dustin. It's better to be like Donna. People like Donna are often happier, and sometimes it appears luck is always on their side as opportunities seem to consistently be put in their path. My friends feel this way about me. For example, while writing this book we reserved an apartment in Toronto. My husband had mentioned to the owner that we were coming to town to give me the opportunity to write my book. Upon hearing that, he upgraded us to a room with an amazing view. Some may consider this luck. It's not. I'm blessed, blessed because my intuition is flowing and I'm in resonance with the universe. Individuals who are able to see through their experiences, both good and bad, and purposefully choose their actions will find "luck."

Finding the blessings may prove challenging to you at this moment in time. You may feel as though you either have a dark cloud following you, that you have bad karma to work through or that you have been cursed. Every experience likely feels negative. If this is you, you are not alone. Unfortunately, there are more of these individuals in the world than those that feel blessed. And it is understandable why this would be the case. Horrible things do happen. Babies are murdered for no apparent reason. Good people get sick and die too young. Countries go to war. This list can go on and on. For those who have experienced many atrocities and pains in their life, it causes them to question the existence of God. Why would God or the universe want good people to suffer? That philosophical question is too big to be addressed in this book. What I will address here is the fact that negative experiences can be used to open your intuition and manifest your heart's desires. In fact, this is the strongest tool you as an intuitive and manifestor have in your tool kit.

You may be asking yourself why is it that negative experiences bring about intuition and spirituality? There are several reasons. First, after a trauma an individual seeks understanding and the purpose behind why the bad event occurred. Why do we do that? We live in a society that embraces the cause-effect relationship theory, and as a result we believe there is reason for everything. But finding a reason isn't easy. Consider Fatima. While she is a generous woman, she is miserable. She has suffered domestic abuse, filed bankruptcy (twice), endured significant health problems during a pregnancy which caused her to almost lose her daughter, and in the course of one year been in four car accidents. Her quest for understanding the reason for these hardships has gone unanswered which has left her bitter. Her response to, *"Everything happens for a reason,"* is always, *"That's BS."* She has lost her faith and struggles to find the good in situations. Is this you? Or, would you classify yourself as being more like myself. After a serious accident, I searched my soul for why it occurred. Today, I believe the accident allowed me to be on my spiritual path. Had it not been for the accident, I would likely be a scientist conducting research and not doing the spiritual work I do today. The accident put me on the path I am on today. This rationale may or may not be true; unfortunately, a better understanding won't come until I get to the other side, but the rationale makes me feel better in this moment. You may be no different. Finding peace and acceptance after a damaging experience leads you to a broader understanding, an understanding that often comes from the heart not the head.

    Another reason spirituality and intuition are broadened after undesirable circumstances is that individuals often begin to see the world differently. This is most easily explained by an example of death. My husband lost his father at the age of ten; his father was thirty-eight. This traumatic event caused my husband to look at the world very differently. He knew from a young age that he wasn't invincible, and his innocence was lost. My husband thought he had dealt with and processed his father's death, until he hit his thirty-eighth year, which proved to be challenging for him. Why? Because he realized he was about to outlive his father and his own mortality became apparent again. It also caused him to look at the world in a very different manner and in doing so, his intuition flourished. He felt closer to his father than he had ever felt before. He also found a deeper peace with the trauma than he'd ever experienced before.

A final reason why unpleasant situations open your intuition is that they may bring you closer to God. This is most commonly experienced by individuals who recount a near death experience. Individuals that have had a near death experience in that moment of death have returned to the creator, heaven, the universe, whatever you choose to call it. By returning, they again become one with God. They are filled with love, knowledge and a knowing. Very often the person has a greater sense of purpose, but I have also witnessed this revelation with individuals who are involved with domestic abuse. Julie is an example of this. She and her boyfriend had been together more than two years and he beat her almost every day: sometimes with his hands, other times with his fists, and still others with whatever object was handy. As she tells it, the day she decided to leave she had a peace and clarity she had not felt in years. Despite the challenges she knew she would face, she had the feeling it was going to be all right. She said after that the whispers from her intuition were strong. And she is grateful to her inner voice as she feels that directed her path.

All of these are reasons why negative events cause an individual to seek and understand their intuition and spirituality more. As you reflect on the unpleasant experiences, it's not the event itself that is important, but rather how you perceive it. As mentioned earlier, I have been told, *"Dawn, you live a blessed life. You are lucky."* It's not luck so much as it is perception. I look for the opportunity. That doesn't mean it's easy. There are times I ask, *"Why is this happening?"* When I start to feel sorry for myself, I immediately remind myself that it's because there must be something better coming. When I believe that, there always is. Take for example my job. When I left the job with the controlling boss, Andrea, I thought I had a job lined up. The Executive Director of the organization had all but promised me the job. When she scheduled the interview with the Board Chair, she assured me it was protocol. When she then called and informed me the organization had selected another candidate, I was stunned. Not getting that job, however, was a blessing. It allowed me to do the work I love.

When a negative experience happens to you, what do you do? Do you mourn it? Do you get upset? Do you blame yourself? Or consider what you could have done differently? Do you stew? Or do you celebrate what you have and what may be coming? If you don't do this, try it. You'll be surprised what you find. For example, my husband and I went to one of our favorite restaurants. He was looking forward to the Chilean sea bass. It is his favorite. Unfortunately, after ordering it the server had the uncomfortable job of informing him the restaurant was out of the fish. Devastated, he asked the server for a few minutes. He was ready to leave. I told him that it was an opportunity to try something new as he always ordered the sea bass. Begrudgingly he decided on the beef wellington. Turns out he was glad he did. He commented it was the most tender cut of beef he ever had. Had the restaurant not been out of fish, he would have never had it. What might the universe have in store for you? If you are willing to look, and more importantly evolve, you will likely be amazed.

CHAPTER TWELVE
TRAGEDY

"Life is a tragedy when seen in close-up, but a comedy in the long-shot. To truly laugh, you must be able to take your pain, and play with it!"
Charlie Chaplin

It has been my experience that most seekers of spirituality, be it experienced mediums and healers or "newbies," will tell you that their journey began as a result of a traumatic event. The hardship may have been a death, a near death experience, a health crisis or some other tragedy. The trauma is unique to each individual, but what is universal is that after the event the world stopped making sense. The individual is confused and often asks the question, *"Why did this happen?"* or *"What did I do to deserve this?"* He or she is often unable to find a logical explanation. When faced with tragedy, some refuse to grow and instead wallow and grieve the past. Wallowing is not the path the seeker takes; instead, he or she chooses to see the misfortune as an opportunity and grows from it. Many come to the belief that an underlying reason exists and he or she doesn't have the ability to understand why yet. This results in a spiritual peace for some and for some it inspires a desire to know more. That desire to learn leads individuals to spiritual classes and intuition.

As I mentioned, it has been my experience that a traumatic event brings people to spirituality. All of my students have had an experience. For Kaitlyn it was the day she gave birth to her son Asher. The birth was riddled with complications that almost resulted in the death of her and the baby. For Ashley, a member of the Air Force, it was the day a bomb exploded behind her. The day her younger brother died in a tragic car accident caused Taylor to want to understand more. Every individual has a story. I am not exempt. Despite being raised in a family that was supportive of my spirituality, it wasn't until after a life changing event that my spirituality and intuition were truly embraced and came to fruition.

My experience occurred on Monday, February 4, 2002 at approximately 11:30 am. I was a first semester senior at Allegheny College. That day I skipped my morning classes to trek to Erie, PA as my oboe had been in for repair and I needed it for orchestra rehearsal that afternoon. It was a little snowy when I started my drive, but nothing I was concerned about. I was just twenty-one years old and felt invincible. I also felt I could handle the snow having grown up in Buffalo!

During the drive to Erie, I was taken aback as the roads were snowier than I anticipated. The drive that typically took thirty minutes took me about forty-five that morning. I was relieved when I arrived at the repair shop and commented to the manager, *"Be careful. It's a little slick out there!"* Those words have haunted me for they were a harbinger for what was to come.

I breathed a sigh of relief as I walked out of the store as the snow seemed to be letting up. I hoped the snow letting up meant my drive back to Allegheny would be smoother than my ride to Erie. Unfortunately, it wasn't. The further south on 79 I went, the heavier the snow bands became. As I approached the Edinboro exit, I contemplated pulling off, but there weren't many places to stop and while I had skipped my morning classes, I didn't want to skip the afternoon classes as well. As a result, I continued my journey and flipped on my flashers knowing I should be cautious and go slow.

It was the longest drive of my life and I found myself continuously looking at the clock. Just when I didn't think I could make it any further, I saw the exit for Saegertown. Relief rushed over me as this meant that in less than ten miles, I'd be safe and sound back at school. It also meant I'd also be back in time for my afternoon classes.

I never made it those last ten miles. Shortly after seeing the sign, my life was forever changed. Two 18-wheeler trucks came up behind me and lost control, pinning my car, a Nissan Altima, between them. With nowhere to go, my pinned car slid under one of the trucks and in doing so the top of the vehicle was sheared off. As my car spun around like a pinball, it hit a truck that had pulled over to the side of the road due to the inclement weather and ricocheted back into traffic. After making a few more circles, my car finally came to a stop. Before the accident concluded, my battered car took one more assault. A flat-bed carrying industrial metal piping had been one of the vehicles to lose control, and the momentum of the accident caused the truck's bed to tip. The load of metal pipes landed squarely on my now roofless car crushing it.

My memories of that accident are a blur. I remember seeing the Saegertown exit sign, a gold light and then nothing at all. For the longest time I believed the gold light was headlights from a car that lost control ahead of me. I believed that was the cause of the accident. I was insistent. I believed it in every cell of my body. But I was wrong. While there were about a dozen vehicles in the accident, none were gold. Additionally, I couldn't have seen headlights. According to witnesses and the expert who conducted an accident investigation, the accident began as a result of trucks behind me not ahead of me.

I'm blessed to be alive. I'm also blessed that my recollections of the experience are vague and jumbled. My memories of the accident itself are limited to a vision of my bloody hand reaching up through the pipes calling for help and exclaiming more to God than the responders, "*I'm not going to die*"; a woman who shared my hospital room who kept me company as I waited for loved ones; and, a gold light. Even though I have these memories, I don't trust they are truly mine. Instead, I believe these are my ego's desire to remember, which has fabricated a story to bring me inner peace. I say this because while I have the memories, they feel more like a story than a memory. In fact, I know some of the stories aren't accurate as I had a room in the emergency room all to myself.

Not having horrific memories of the accident is a gift, but it is not the only one. Another godsend is that no one else involved in the pile-up was injured and considering the beating my car and I took it was a miracle I escaped with only minor injuries. If I didn't believe in miracles before, I do now. Looking back, I could have been beheaded. I wasn't. I could have been crushed. I wasn't. In fact, I didn't break a single bone, nor did I suffer internal bleeding.

That didn't mean I walked away scot-free. I looked like a monster. My eyes were black as the pressure from the pipes and trauma caused all the blood vessels in them to burst. My face was bloody and swollen. Due to the shattered windshield and metal shards from my car and the piping, hospital staff were tasked with getting glass pieces out of my eyes and open wounds. My eyes were flushed. Chunks of metal and glass were tenderly picked out of a laceration that left the jaw bone exposed and stretched from my left ear to the left corner of my mouth. After removing the fragments, a doctor gingerly stitched the wound and applied tape and liquid stitches to the many other cuts upon my face.

The college, my sorority and my mother were notified of the accident. Several of my sorority sisters showed up, offered their support and sat with me for several hours as we waited for my mother to arrive from Buffalo.

When she did, the hospital wasted no time. While I couldn't be discharged into my own care due to medical concerns, within minutes of my mother's arrival I was discharged into her care. Despite the significant head injury, the hospital had concluded there was no need to admit or even keep me overnight for observation. In fact, the staff hadn't informed my mother or me regarding tests that had been run, the results or next steps in treatment. Confused and not knowing what to say, the only thing my mother could think to ask is, *"Does she have a concussion?"* She was even more surprised when staff retorted, *"Of course. Look at her."*

I was in pain and somewhat delusional at this point. My mother was terrified for my health, as she was a nurse and knew that concussions were serious business. She knew that making the two-hour drive home with few hospitals between Meadville and Buffalo was risky. And from looking at my current status, she knew that my health could go south at any time. She was also concerned because it was close to 10 o'clock at night and her drive down 79 hadn't been much better than my own. In fact, she was concerned that it may be worse because it hadn't stopped snowing and both sides of traffic were being detoured as crews continued to clean the highway up. With that in mind, she asked the ER staff if she could have a few minutes to call local hotels to arrange a room for the night as she didn't want to make the drive but rather felt it smart to observe me throughout the night. Begrudgingly the staff agreed.

Fortunately, a local hotel had a room and she monitored my condition there throughout the night. Soon as the sun came up the next morning, my mother got me in the car and drove home to Buffalo. Not trusting the care received in the hospital, she immediately made an appointment with my primary care physician. My primary care physician gave me a once over and sent me home. In significant pain, I was taken to our local emergency room for more tests. In the next few weeks, I was in the doctor's office at least once a week, often being told it would take time to heal.

When I reflect on the months following the accident, all I recall is being in constant pain. My head throbbed. My memory was shot. I would lose words. My vision was blurry. My balance was off. After a few of months of being told, *"It's a really bad head injury, it takes time,"* my mother was frustrated with my physician as she didn't see me making any progress. It was at that point she followed her intuition and made an appointment with a neurologist. The neurologist was aghast with the treatment thus far and immediately referred me to neurological rehabilitation which consisted of occupational, speech and physical therapy. Unfortunately, the site closest to my home had a waiting list several months long, but the site a half hour away had an opening. The neurologist recommended I start there immediately and when the spot near my home opened, I could transfer. In her opinion, time was of the essence.

Despite the inconvenience, we did it. Therapy became my full-time job. Once I was able to transfer to the clinic near my home, I went to therapy five days a week. After the initial assessments, the occupational therapist discovered significant visual impairments. Upon her recommendation, my mother made an appointment for evaluation with an optometrist that specialized in vision therapy for children and adults with head injuries. As the optometrist conducted his assessment, he discovered my visual field was significantly diminished. To assist my recovery, he recommended specialized vision therapy.

The various therapies lasted more than a year. It was hard work. It was exhausting. The therapy made me sick. Despite the struggles, I look back and know I was blessed. I had a supportive family, especially in the form of my mother and aunt. If it weren't for them advocating for the best care possible and being my voice when I was incapable of speaking up; making, keeping track of and getting me to and from appointments; working with the insurance companies to ensure my medical expenses were covered; and most importantly being my cheerleaders, on both my good days and bad; if it weren't for this and much more, I wouldn't be where I am today. My trauma negatively impacted them, but they stuck by me.

In addition to my family, I was fortunate to have a great team of medical professionals who believed I could have a life again. They fought for the services they believed would assist my recovery. They were compassionate and understood the struggles I was facing. Most importantly, they offered hope when I couldn't see the light and wouldn't allow me to give up on myself. I was blessed to have them on my team.

Today, I see the positive aspects of the accident. At the time, I didn't. I struggled with depression. Like many who have terrible things happen to them, I struggled to understand *"why me?"* and *"what did I do to deserve this?"* While in that dark place, life looked bleak. I couldn't see a future and many days I didn't want to get out of bed. There were times I allowed the negativity to overcome me, and I hurt more. I felt powerless.

Despite the uncertainty. Despite the hurt. I didn't want the pain or the position I found myself to be in to be my destiny. It was during that time two events served as catalysts that empowered me to take control over my life.

The first statement came from a judge. Due to the accident and my inability to work, medical personnel and my lawyer advised my parents that I should apply for disability. My lawyer compiled the paperwork and submitted it to the state. After being denied, he appealed the decision which resulted in a court hearing. As my memory was still hit or miss, the proceedings are blurry. One moment, however, is as clear as if it had happened yesterday. During my testimony, the judge made the following statement, *"You are 24 years old, do you realize if I grant you disability you won't have to work a day in your life? You'd be a drain on society?"* My lawyer objected, contending the judge was out of line. I burst into tears. I had been ignorant of what being granted disability meant. I was there because it was what my team advised, and I wasn't thinking on my own. The insinuations from the judge crushed me in a worse way than the accident had. My family had instilled a work ethic and had insisted I become a productive member of society. Hearing those words was a defining moment. I decided no matter what it took, I was going to prove the judge wrong. I wasn't going to allow his perception to define me.

That same determination revealed itself in my optometrist's office. After months of vision therapy, my progress was reviewed, and I was disappointed it wasn't where either of us had hoped it would be. The fields of my vision were still limited to a point where I would be unable to drive. Worse, I was still suffering debilitating migraines. After reviewing the results, he regretfully informed me, *"I've done everything I can. The rest is in God's hands."* I'd been through so much at that time his comment didn't sit well with me. How could there be nothing left to do? How could I just give up? Unwilling to accept defeat, his comment prompted me to explore spiritual healing and alternative modalities further.

The accident was the experience, but the comments were the turning point. They caused me to move from a passive participant who was idly watching my life pass me by to one who was directing her own reality. The shift probably occurred because the comments made me mad. They conflicted with my idea of who and what I wanted to be. I was defiant. I was angry. I was provoked. I was determined to change. Unfortunately, the negative experiences we face provoke us to change, if we choose to. Sometimes we must get angry or hit rock bottom to incite change. You also have to believe with all that you are that you can create change in your life.

I believed. My health care providers may not have. My neurologist encouraged me to not get discouraged if I struggled returning to school. My speech pathologist engaged me in volunteer work to demonstrate that there was more to life than the jobs I once dreamed of. There were family members who didn't think I had a chance and spoke of half-way homes. I didn't care, I believed in myself.

My determination incited change. I was unhappy with my set of circumstances and didn't care for the trajectory others saw for me, so I chose to change it. Some believe it was luck. It wasn't. It was hard work, sprinkled with blessings from the universe. I chose to push through the headaches and go outside my comfort zone.

You can choose to do the same thing. Little changes in your life create big ripples. After deciding not to be defined by my circumstances, the next decision I made was to find joy. Some days that joy consisted of enjoying a glass of red wine and quieting my mind. Other days it was the comfort my pug Daphne brought me. There was joy in my life, I just had to find it. As I embraced those little joys, more came. I was able to afford my own apartment, and not only did I hold down a job but due to my success, was promoted. I eventually found love, graduated from college, bought a home, was able to run a successful business and have a child. These were all experiences that at one time they questioned whether I would be possible.

As I mentioned, my story isn't unique. Every individual has lived through and triumphed over conflict. You probably have one of your own. In fact, it might be what incited you to pick up this book. Turn your attention to your experiences. Consider the traumas in your life. Narrow them down to one that caused you to look at the world differently and that pivotally changed you.

Questions to Consider

Of all the traumas you experienced, why did you choose this one?

How did the circumstances conflict with the beliefs you held about yourself and the goals you had for your life?

How did you empower yourself in this situation?

Most importantly, what did you learn?

How does this trauma continue to affect you today?

The accident caused me to recognize I am stronger than I believed. It also caused me to seek a deeper spirituality. Did your trauma do the same thing? Additionally, I approach situations differently. I choose to find joy. What about you? Have you chosen to find joy in the situation? If not, what positive experiences have you had as a result of the incident? Do you choose joy every day? If not, it's time to find a way.

Traumas teach you to find blessings in unexpected places. That is the universal lesson you are meant to learn. Once you learn that, while you may have hardship, the traumas are few and far between. To demonstrate, let's look at Georgia's story.

Georgia is a two-time cancer survivor who found out that after ten years the cancer had spread again. Determined not to be defined as a sick cancer patient, she asked her doctors not to share her stage of diagnosis or prognosis. Instead, she wished to focus on her health and recovery. While undergoing treatment, she never asked *"Why me?"* Instead, she asked, *"What do I have to learn?"* Upon asking that question, she knew her lesson was she needed to take care of herself and not worry about others.

As a school teacher, mother of five, grandmother to two and friend to many, this was a hard lesson. While Georgia wanted to continue to help everyone solve their problems, this conflicted with her insight. Taking the insight seriously, during her treatments she took a step away from her family's obstacles and focused on her healing. While receiving chemo, rather than babysitting her grandchildren and mediating family arguments, she let them figure it out. She also asked her kids for help. To her great joy they stepped up. They drove her to chemo, took her to Boston to see one of the top oncologists in the country, prepared meals for her and cleaned her home. She graciously accepted their assistance.

Having cancer for a third time has not been easy. She is a strong woman, but she was terrified. The chemo and radiation affected her more significantly than ever before. She is fearful, but intuitively she knows she is going to make it. Despite that, she has asked on more than a dozen occasions, *"Dawn, do you really think I'm going to be ok?"* Each time I can confidently say, *"YES"* for I clearly see her dancing away at her granddaughter's wedding. When I say that, she tears up and often responds, *"I do too."* And while she wouldn't say she is grateful to have cancer again, she sees the growth in herself and those she loves. She sees the blessings. One of the biggest blessings, the cancer responded better to treatment than expected and the cancer has gone back into remission.

Miracles happen when you look past the fear and believe they can. For Georgia, this was a miracle. She was already a spiritual person, but this has caused her spirituality to run deeper and her ability to manifest become greater. When you look at the traumas in your life, look at the lessons you've learned. The miracles that have been given.

CHAPTER THIRTEEN
DEATH

"The fear of death is only the consciousness of unresolved contradictions of life."
Leo Tolstoy

Traumas come in all shapes and sizes, including the death of a loved one. Each of us will lose people we love. You may have already, perhaps a parent, child, family member or friend. If you haven't been impacted at this point, you are fortunate. But death is inevitable, everyone dies. At some point someone you care for deeply is going to pass and when he or she does, it is going to change you. You may feel loneliness, regret, helplessness or perhaps even relief. Your feelings through the loss will be unique, but the experience is universal. For that reason, death is being explored specifically. Death is also being called out as it often leads to questions about spirituality which can lead the seeker to peace and enhanced intuition.

If you have experienced the death of a loved one, there is a litany of questions you may be asking yourself. If the person passed tragically like my grandmother and three aunts who died in a house fire, you may ask yourself, "*Why were they taken so young?*" and lament over the loss. If the loved one didn't die tragically but instead endured a progressive, long, and painful decline due to disease like my aunt with cancer, you may ask yourself, *"Why does God allow such suffering?"* The emptiness you experience due to the passing may lead you to question the existence of a spiritual realm or heaven. The list of questions goes on and on. Unfortunately, on the physical plane of existence the questions will remain unanswered. Our human mind cannot comprehend the vastness of the spiritual realm.

The lack of answers brings continual pain for some. Felicia is an example of this. She has lost two husbands and a son to cancer. Her first husband passed in his mid-twenties, less than a month after their daughter was born; her second husband passed in his early forties; and her son passed in his early thirties, leaving behind a nine and four-year-old. Felicia knows the emptiness left and the subsequent pain experienced due to the loss of a loved one never go away. Due to the continual heartache and grief, she cannot comprehend a reason a benevolent God would subject anyone to this pain. Unfortunately, that pain seeps out and influences every relationship she has. She cycles through friends and is frequently estranged from at least one family member.

Fortunately, you don't have to be like Felicia. The death of a loved one does not need to cause you continual pain; it can lead to hope. That is not to say hope takes the emptiness and pain away. You will still miss your loved one as no person, possession or experience can fill that void. Faith will bring you peace knowing your loved one is in a place of unconditional love and that upon your passing you will be reunited. It can also lead you to your intuition. Let's consider Mary. She was only twenty when she lost her father to cancer. During the last year of his life, Mary traveled back and forth from college in Texas to her home in New York to help care for her ailing father. This was the most painful period in her life, for not only was she losing her father, she was also confronted with her spiritual beliefs. She didn't want to believe in mediums, as she couldn't see the evidence with her own two eyes. After her father's passing, however, she couldn't deny the existence of an afterlife as inexplicable experiences happened every day. She would find coins in places they should not be, songs special to her father would play on the radio when she was missing him, and while traveling abroad with her siblings they were amazed that the spaghetti they ordered on his birthday tasted exactly like their father's sauce. While she doesn't understand why her father was taken from her and experiences significant sadness knowing he missed her college graduation and will miss significant moments in her life such as her wedding day, she has faith that he is around and that at some point they will meet again.

Being Mary isn't easy. In fact, after the death of a loved one most of us will be like Felicia. You will go through the stages of grief and will experience anger and/or depression. The goal, however, is to move to acceptance. Your perspective facilitates that.

Moving to acceptance, while challenging, has always been easier for me as death was discussed in my household and as a result, from an early age, I knew and perhaps more importantly accepted that everyone died. Death was a topic for a variety of reasons. For one, my mother, a nurse, provided home care to dying individuals. I knew when she started caring for a new patient it was because the prior one had passed. Additionally, several family members had passed before I was ten. This included my great grandparents, an uncle and even a cousin. Understanding these losses was important, not only for my personal comprehension but also to be sensitive to the experience of my family members. For example, I was aware that my aunt and uncle steered clear of alcohol because their son was killed by a drunk driver. When the movie *Drop Dead Fred* was released, despite it being one of my favorites, I was reminded that it would be insensitive to rent it while visiting with cousins as the father they lost was named Fred. Additionally, having been named after my mother's youngest sister who died in the house fire, I was aware that people live on in a variety of ways. They live on in memories, our actions designed to honor the deceased, and in spirit. Because my grandfather knew I saw spirit, he discussed death and the eternal nature of the spirit. These conversations regarding death were critical to the development of my intuition.

While death was discussed, it wasn't until I was twelve that I truly began to understand its implications. In the spring of my sixth-grade year a classmate, Allison, died. This was when death became real. I'd known Allison since kindergarten, half my life at that point. This was our first year in middle school, and Allison and I were on the same "team," which meant we shared the same group of teachers and had some classes together. We were both somewhat awkward, so due to the shared history we gravitated towards one another while at school and often ate lunch together. Despite knowing each other for years, our friendship was confined to the school walls.

The last time I saw Allison alive was the Friday before Spring Break. She was a moody middle schooler, and she was in quite the mood that day. During lunch she had an argument with those of us at the lunch table. I don't recall what the disagreement was about, but it was insignificant, like who was the better musical group, En Vogue or Salt-N-Pepa. Despite being insignificant, the disagreement resulted in Allison storming off to sit at a table by herself. As I sat looking at her in isolation, I felt sorrow for her loneliness and had an ominous gut-wrenching feeling that something awful was going to happen. But I was twelve and not adept at tapping into my intuition; I didn't know what that feeling meant. In hindsight, even if I had been proficient, I still may not have known what was to come.

When I reflect on the day, I know that I could not have done anything to save her. I regret that I never acted on that ominous feeling and I did not apologize or encourage Allison to rejoin us. Instead, I continued lunch with my friends and allowed Allison to sit at the lunch table unaccompanied. I also didn't invite her to come sit with us after lunch when we returned to a large classroom to finish the movie we were watching. I wish I had because it would have allowed me to say goodbye or give her a kind word. Instead, shortly after lunch I joined my Odyssey of the Mind team, excited for a competition in Binghamton, NY that weekend.

On Sunday afternoon after the competition, my family arrived back in Buffalo. I was disappointed with a loss but was looking forward to the week off school. To my family's surprise, our answering machine was blinking with more than two dozen messages. Rarely seeing that many messages, my mother knew the messages were important and immediately began listening. The first message was from my best friend's mother, Jane. Upon hearing the urgency in Jane's voice, instead of listening to all the messages she turned off the machine and immediately dialed Jane to find out what had happened. I didn't need to hear more. The gut-wrenching pain I felt Friday afternoon returned. I knew Allison was dead.

Jane confirmed Allison's death. On Friday afternoon, Allison had been walking around town after school. This was typical, but that afternoon while trying to scoot past a parking lot entrance she was hit by a car. She hadn't seen the car and the driver hadn't seen her. She died instantaneously.

I didn't have the maturity or the emotional intelligence necessary to fully process the significance of her death. I was filled with guilt. I was filled with fear. I was full of confusion. This was the first death of someone I knew and was close to. Not only that, it was the first time seeing a dead body. I was surprised with how she looked. The trauma was apparent, her face was swollen and even with makeup her face was blue. It was odd seeing her body in the coffin, dressed in a plaid baby doll dress she'd worn only weeks before. I also was uncomfortable as her spirit stood with her mother and father in the receiving line. Her spirit, however, didn't speak, which confused me further. I wondered if she were still mad at me? She didn't feel mad, but she also didn't feel like the other spirits I'd encountered. Her energy was heavier.

I was full of questions and grief. I don't remember exactly what my parents said, but I remember they consoled and helped me reconcile my feelings of guilt and fear. My grandfather assured me that she was around because that's what spirits do: they visit people they love. Older and wiser now, I understand that after a person dies, he or she typically "hangs around" for at least his or her funeral or memorial service, sometimes longer. Some may call them "earth bound." That's why Allison felt heavier.

Just as I was wrapping my head around Allison's death, a whole new set of questions arose. I began to wonder why, if we can still "*call Allison up now and again,*" were my classmates and teachers distraught? At the time, I saw Allison's death in the same manner I viewed a classmate moving to Tennessee the year before. It was then that it became very evident to me that not everyone could see spirit. Anytime I made a comment about Allison's passing, teachers and students responded with concern and sometimes anger. My Math teacher would snap at me. My Science teacher, the self-assigned lead teacher, took an entire class period to deliver a potent message informing her students that she understood we were having a hard time processing Allison's death, but grief doesn't permit students to tell lies, make up tall tales or speak ill of the dead. She informed the class that Allison was an obedient,

Catholic girl who would be welcomed by the angels into heaven. She would not go to hell or hang around in purgatory as a ghost. That doesn't happen. Furthermore, she would not permit any more whisperings or discussions about her death. She informed the class that guidance counselors were on hand should any of us feel the need to talk to someone. During the entire speech, I felt she was staring at me and I had to restrain myself from bursting into tears. I didn't understand how my teacher's perspective could vary so dramatically from not only what I'd been taught, but also from what I'd experienced. My head spun with questions.

Fortunately, I had a supportive family. My mother and grandfather shared that not everyone holds the same beliefs or has the same experiences we do. I was also encouraged to keep my beliefs to myself being told, *"Dawn, there are three things people shouldn't talk about: religion, politics and money."* With that adage in mind, from that point forward I kept my mouth shut and tried my best to ignore my gift, at least at school.

I walked away from this experience confused and even defeated. The experience haunted me for many years. In high school, Allison's family hosted an exchange student from Italy. I became good friends with the exchange student but could not visit Allison's home or meet with her parents as I still struggled with her passing and felt shame.

Dealing with death is hard and it is complex. It brings fears and core beliefs to the surface. Reconciling those fears and beliefs, especially when impacted by outside factors can be challenging.

Take a moment to consider a significant loss in your life.

> ## Questions to Consider
>
> *Who did you lose? What was their relationship to you?*
>
> *How did he or she pass? Was it sudden? Or did you know his or her death was coming?*
>
> *What feelings did you experience? What emotions do you continue to experience?*
>
> *Why did this death impact you? How did it change you?*
>
> *How did this death impact your spirituality and belief system?*

As you consider these questions, even if you didn't experience significant grief you will find that you were impacted by the loss. For example, I was able to work through the grief of losing a friend quickly. The guilt and confusion created by her death existed until I explored my spirituality after the car accident. It wasn't until I actively sought understanding that it came.

When I actively sought that understanding, I recognized that the manner I chose to respond to her passing significantly impacted my intuition. I shielded myself because I didn't want to experience the negative emotions elicited by her passing and imprinted on me by my science teacher. Upon exploring my spirituality, I have been able to embrace the experience.

With this in mind, reflect back on the death you considered a few moments ago.

> ## Questions to Consider
>
> *Have you moved through the guilt and grief, or have you found that you continue to carry emotional baggage?*
>
> *If you have moved through the guilt and grief, what assisted you in this process?*
>
> *If you have not moved through the guilt and grief, what is holding you back?*
>
> *How is it that you honor the individual who has passed? How would they feel about your feeling their death?*
>
> *How are you better or worse as a result of the passing?*

Through death life lessons are learned. Not only are you confronted with your beliefs regarding what happens to an individual when he or she dies, you may also find yourself questioning your life purpose. It also makes it clear how short life is and that every day is not promised. Your perspective regarding these questions influences the joy to be brought into your life.

CHAPTER FOURTEEN
THE EXPERIENCES

"People grow through experience if they meet life honestly and courageously. This is how character is built."
Eleanor Roosevelt

The traumas and deaths you chose to explore in the previous chapters likely caused you to seek greater understanding. This is not uncommon. It is also not uncommon that when you begin to look for answers, you start to have experiences that have never happened or happened infrequently before. You may start to experience synchronicities and have vivid or precognitive dreams. You may find you are more empathic than before and may even experience inexplicable knowledge. The world may suddenly seem different.

You may have thought you were going crazy. Chances are since you are reading this book, the experiences struck a cord within you and have caused you to dig for a deeper and more robust understanding. You may read books like this one or meet with priests, pastors, rabbis, even psychics and mediums. You may pray for understanding or ask your deceased loved ones for signs. You may even attend healing or mediumship development courses. The journey to comprehension is individual and unique, the reason for the journey is universal. Individuals want to understand. I was no different.

A couple years after the accident, while in the midst of severe depression and struggling to find acceptance, my mom, aunt and I trekked down to Lily Dale to meet with a medium in hopes of obtaining insight. It was a cold day at the end of March and we had appointments to sit with a medium who had come highly recommended. As we pulled through the gates and made our way down the narrow streets, our hearts sang. For the first time in a long time, I was hopeful.

When we reached the medium's home it was decided that I should go first. I was excited but also a little anxious and nervous because besides the palm reading at college, this was my first reading. Family members had shared their experiences from previous readings which caused me to believe my grandfather or grandmother would visit. I hoped they would bring promising insights to my future which from my perspective appeared bleak.

As I walked into the medium's quaint room, I felt transported back in time. The room was outfitted with antique furniture, under each lamp was a delicate doily and lace curtains hung in the windows. The medium closed her eyes and started with a prayer. As anticipated, my grandfather visited that day. To my surprise, however, he was not the first person to step in. The first person to visit was a young man. The reader described him as tall with striking blue/green eyes. She noted he had a sarcastic sense of humor and indicated he had hanged himself. During the reading, I experienced loved-one amnesia and was unable to place this young man. I took the message but thought the reader was bonkers. It wasn't until weeks after the reading that it hit me. The young man had to be Chuck. With this realization, I was overcome with emotion.

Why did Chuck's visit elicit such a potent response, especially considering just weeks before I was unable to place him? It wasn't because of my relationship to Chuck. Chuck and I attended the same college. He and I were friends, but only loosely so. He was a Sigma Alpha Epsilon (SAE), the brother fraternity to ADPi. We had many mutual friends and as a result ended up at many of the same parties and gatherings, but it was only through those mutual friends we interacted. Despite our loose friendship, Chuck and his death crossed my mind often. In fact, Chuck's death caused me a great deal of pain and guilt, albeit irrational. I felt guilt, but not because I believed I could have prevented Chuck's suicide. Prior to his death, he was being treated for mental illness and was under the care of both a psychiatrist and counselor. I knew if they weren't able to prevent his suicide, I as a loose friend had no control. The guilt I carried is best described as survivor's guilt. You see, the accident I was in was one of two tragedies at Allegheny College in February of 2002; Chuck's suicide was the other. That both these tragedies occurred in tandem caused me to internalize his death. His death made my close call and mortality that much more poignant. Irrationally, I questioned *did he die because I lived?* I would ponder the statement, *"the natural order of the universe must be maintained"* and contemplate whether or not my living in some way threw off that balance, since my survival was a miracle after all. When that thought would enter my mind, I would wonder if his death had been the universe creating order.

Those thoughts sound crazy and even in the moment, I knew they were irrational. But that didn't mean the thoughts didn't haunt me. Chuck appearing in my reading and his message offered comfort and allowed me to release long-standing pain and guilt. Chuck spoke to my soul in a way that no one else was able to. Through his message, my spirit began to heal.

I sought out this experience and its subsequent lessons. I chose to consult a medium for insight. And while the experience was not what I anticipated, it was what my soul needed. The universe will always provide you with what you need although it may not always be what you expect. Additionally, there are times as with this experience when it is only after you dig deeper that you recognize the lessons.

Let's take a moment for you to consider times in your life you have sought out life lessons.

Questions to Consider

Is there a book you read that caused you to view the world differently? What was it? How did you change?

Is there a time you sought out guidance from an individual that caused you to look at the world differently? How was it? Why did you reach out to him or her? How did he or she change you?

Are you still learning from this experience?

Why did you choose the example you did? How does this experience continue to impact you today?

Sometimes the experiences are ones we seek. Other times, those experiences are ones that simply cross our path. That was the case with my next example, when I was on a plane to visit my aunt and uncle. It was shortly after being discharged from occupational and speech therapy and I was just beginning my spiritual journey. The trip to my aunt and uncle's was arranged to give my mother much needed rest, and we hoped I would find direction. A "chance" meeting provided just that.

Weather had caused several flights to be canceled, and as a result, my flight was at capacity. Upon boarding, I found I was seated next to a middle-aged gentleman with white hair and warm eyes. It was late, so while I pulled out my book and placed it on my lap, I had no intention of reading but instead planned on taking a nap. That didn't happen. Upon seeing the book in my lap, *Tuesdays with Morrie,* the gentleman struck up conversation. He made note of the book I was clutching, and then gently suggested that I consider reading the *Life of Pi.*

The book had been published several years prior to our meeting, but it had not yet reached my radar. When he explained the allegory, I was intrigued. The conversation flowed effortlessly between the two of us. Through the conversation, I learned he attended a non-denominational spiritual church located not far from where I'd be staying. I had wished to attend the church and classes while visiting but didn't have the opportunity. The two-hour flight seemed to be gone in an instant, and while only a brief meeting, the positive nature of this interaction has stayed with me for more than ten years.

Has there been a time where a chance meeting changed your life? Take time to reflect on a chance encounter.

Questions to Consider

Have you encountered a person that, while the relationship didn't last, the memory did?

Have you experienced a situation that, while seemingly insignificant, has changed you?

Why does this situation linger?

How did this encounter change you?

Sometimes the experiences you have are positive, other times the experiences are uncomfortable. An experience that caused me to be outside my comfort zone occurred during one of my family's yearly pilgrimage to Niagara-on-the-Lake. Niagara-on-the-Lake is a small town just east of Niagara Falls that is known for the Shaw Festival that features plays throughout the summer, a quaint Main Street lined with unique boutiques, picturesque golf courses on the shore of Lake Ontario, and Fort George, an English Fort used during the War of 1812. Since childhood, my family has visited this quaint town to take in the sights and get salted black licorice, a family favorite.

The first annual trip to Niagara-on-the-Lake after the accident was different. I anticipated it would be more challenging as I was plagued with nagging headaches and crowds made my skin crawl. Despite these ailments, I didn't want to miss out. To accommodate my condition, we planned on cutting the trip short and instead of spending a whole day, we planned on only staying a couple of hours. We almost didn't even make it that long. Upon getting out of the car, I was immediately hit with a sensation I had never felt before. I felt dizzy, sick to my stomach and overwhelmed with sadness. These sensations caused me concern and confusion as none of the triggers that often brought on these symptoms were present. It was an overcast day, so the sun wasn't bothering my eyes. We had parked on a side street, so I hadn't yet experienced the Main Street crowds. Moments before I had been filled with anticipation and excitement for the day. I couldn't figure out why I was suddenly feeling ill. In that moment, I was determined to at least get my licorice and decided to ignore the feelings. As I indignantly marched down the street, as quickly as the ailments came on, they passed.

I dismissed my experience in Niagara-on-the-Lake at first. That only lasted a short amount of time but as occurrences like the one above began to occur more frequently, I became concerned. Filled with unease, I shared the puzzling ailments with my medical providers. In an attempt to minimize the symptoms, my medications increased. More medication led to new symptoms and the occurrences the medications were prescribed to "cure" didn't stop. Discouraged that my symptoms were getting worse and questioning the efficacy of the medication, my mental health counselor felt the symptoms might have an emotional and/or spiritual root. Believing this to be true, she encouraged me to read several spiritual books. She gave me, *When Bad Things Happen to Good People* by Harold Kushner and *You Can Heal Your Life* by Louise Hay.

These books intrigued me. They caused me to look at my situation from a different perspective. With lots of time on my hands, I began researching spiritual healing and intuition. I read everything I could get my hands on, from Sylvia Browne to John Edwards to obscure books like Howard Storm's *Descent into Death*. I hoped that one of these books would help me understand my experiences, and perhaps even offer a remedy to my predicament that had eluded traditional medical providers.

It is at this point in my students' lives that I meet them. They've had the a-ha moment and now they are experiencing the world differently. Not only that, they've done some research on the topic, but they need something more. This very well may be where you are in your story. If this is where you are, you are in a great place. You are exploring and creating a new story. And you have a choice. Do you run and hide? Or do you face these experiences head on? The manner by which you face these occurrences defines who you are.

The lesson I learned was that I couldn't run away from the experiences. I was becoming overwhelmed, anxious, experienced headaches and body aches everywhere I went. For peace of mind, I had to have an escape route no matter where I went. When I'd walk into an unfamiliar location, I sized up the facility and immediately took note of the exits. I had a plan for the minimum amount of time I would stay. If it was a place I couldn't leave, I identified areas for retreat that would allow me to catch my breath. I would choose the time I attended places carefully. Ironically, many of these things I still do. My husband and I don't go out for dinner between 6 and 7pm, instead we try to go between 4:30 and 5:30pm to avoid the crowds. We have a time we shoot for. But it has allowed us to live our lives. For example, when we recently visited Disney World, my goal was to make it to the Move It! Shake It! Dance Party at 5:45pm. We ended up staying until fireworks, but after that parade we were ready to go anytime. Understanding your limitations and working within your confines will help you tremendously.

In addition to living within your confines, embracing these limitations and/or new experiences is important as well. For example, the experience in Niagara-on-the-Lake was just one of many. I had a similar experience in Gettysburg, Pa; during a significant storm, as the wind howled and ice caused branches to crash, a sound that reminded me of thundering drums reverberated in my head; I'd meet an individual and have insight like I've never had before; I was drawn to lecture series that opened my eyes. Each of these experiences I embraced, and I spoke to anyone who would listen about them.

I was amazed with the number of people I encountered during my spiritual evolution. It seemed that everywhere I went, I met someone new who had new information to share that expanded my understanding. For example, while visiting my father who was in Florida for business, he arranged for me to meet with a woman. This woman discussed psychic protection and provided me with tools such as creating a bubble and shielding. Looking back on the experience, I am amazed. It was my father who arranged this encounter. The father who was afraid of my experience as a child. This meeting demonstrated his support and understanding, perhaps if he didn't even realize it.

Encounters like that paved the way for me, so I encourage you to go outside your comfort zone and make experiences like these for yourself. They will facilitate growth. And, more importantly, you will demonstrate that you are not alone.

DEUX

SECTION TWO
MANIFEST YOUR DREAMS

DEUX

CHAPTER FIFTEEN
YOUR STORY

"The more you know of your history, the more liberated you are."
Maya Angelou

Throughout the book the many factors that influence the development of your identity and unique perspectives have been explored. You received an uninhibited glimpse into my life as I shared my experiences as examples. In addition, numerous questions were posed to assist you in your own self-reflection and discovery. If you haven't delved into your story, I encourage you to go back and review those questions now. For ease, the questions have been compiled in the Appendix.

It is important to note, as you evolve your story will change since the perspective you have is a reflection of who you are at any given moment of time. For example, if you were to ask me ten years ago if I would have a child, my response would be a resoundingly loud *"NO."* At the time, I was in a high stress position and couldn't imagine myself taking on the responsibility of raising a child. After leaving the position, my life became more balanced. The freedom my new lifestyle afforded allowed me to entertain the possibility of motherhood. The change in my perspective shocked my colleagues and even some family members. In fact, the dramatic change in mindset led some to believe my pregnancy was unintended. It wasn't. Circumstances changed and so did my perspective. Today I can't imagine my life without my daughter.

As you reflect, you may find the same to be true. In fact, I hope for you it is. Change in perspective is a blessing as it demonstrates personal growth and evolution. Our lives are not meant to be static, rather the encounters and experiences we have every day should and do impact our view of the world. These new experiences, much like the past, will consciously (or unconsciously) cement the beliefs held or assist in further growth and evolution. We can and do change. I am a different version of myself compared to the person who started writing this book, just as you are a different person now as compared to who you were when you started reading it. This concept is liberating in that it means you are not doomed to continue to relive your experience or remain trapped in unhealthy paradigms. You are not what happened to you; instead, you can chart your own path and manifest your desires.

At this point, you should realize that your experiences do affect your current behaviors, but you may still be questioning why knowing your story is so vital. Consider this: *your thoughts become your words which become your actions, your beliefs, and ultimately, your truths*. If this is true, which I believe it is, your thoughts manifest the opportunities that arise in your life. This concept is the premise of the Law of Attraction, which simply asserts that by focusing on positive or negative experiences an individual brings positive or negative experiences into his or her life. Simply put, you will often get what you expect in life. For example, if you are an athlete who is starting for the first time, you may be worried you are going to screw up and disappoint the team. If this is your belief, chances are good that you will make an error and perform below your ability, whereas if you have butterflies but are determined to go out and do your best, despite any errors, you will perform as anticipated, if not better. Are you skeptical? If you are, test the theory out for yourself. Take a day and observe how your behavior impacts those around you. Do this by consciously being kind to everyone you encounter. For example, while at the local coffee shop getting your morning coffee leave a generous tip and say thank you to the barista; or, while checking out at the grocery store make eye contact with and smile at the cashier; or, extend the proverbial olive branch to a coworker you are uncomfortable with by saying hello and inquiring about a topic he or she is passionate about (i.e. kids, specific cause, etc.). As you emit kindness, you will be amazed how it comes back in return. The Law of Attraction works.

Whether you conduct the Law of Attraction exercise or not, and, whether you believe in the Law of Attraction or not, the theory, which I believe to be natural law, is impacting you. You, consciously or unconsciously, are continuously emitting energy. If you are happy, you are exuding happiness and more likely to attract joy; whereas if you are annoyed, you are more likely to be attracting situations that rile you up further. The feelings you have in any moment are informed by not only the immediate circumstances, but as demonstrated, your past experiences and subsequent internal dialogue. If you are unconscious of this dialogue and your motivations, you may be unaware of how it is impacting your external actions. Consider this example: one day my husband was particularly irritable. He stomped around the house with a puss on his face. He snapped at me. I didn't take it personally. He was gruff with our daughter. In response, she became fussy and was less compliant with his requests. When she needed help on the potty, she shut the door on him and called for me. As he tried to get her into her pajamas, she complained and gave him a hard time. The more she resisted him, the more frustrated he became, and the cycle worsened. Witnessing this cycle, I casually asked him if anything happened that day. He snapped no. Knowing that something had to have set him off, I pressed further and queried what he'd done during the day. After some hesitation, he shared he spoke to his mother. I asked how she was and then inquired, "That's what set you off, isn't it?" He stopped dead in his tracks, his eyes became wide, his face became red and his belly expanded like he was about to yell. Instantly, it was as if a pin had struck his belly and deflated it. His energy changed and the irritability he'd been exhibiting diminished. Soon as he became aware of his trigger, he stopped emitting frustration and just as quickly our daughter stopped giving him a hard time and crawled into his lap.

If you are unaware of your story, you may be like my husband and attracting less than desirable outcomes. Becoming aware of that energy, while you may still have the knee-jerk response, you may be able to stop the behavior and redirect towards more positive outcomes.

This is true even if you are not attracting negative experiences into your life as my husband did. Not being aware of your story and the energy you are emitting means you may or may not be working in conjunction with the universe to manifest your life purpose. In fact, you may unwittingly be working against your desires; whereas if you are conscious of the energy you are emitting, it is more likely you will attract your goals.

Information is a powerful tool in the manifestation of one's desires. The more data an individual has the easier it is to make purposeful and informed decisions. In doing so, an individual consistently takes steps towards his or her aspirations. Knowing you story provides you with insights that assist in making those purposeful decisions.

CHAPTER SIXTEEN
WHAT DEUX YOU WANT?

"Knowing what you want is the first step toward getting it."
Mae West

We've talked (a lot) about where you've been and why your story is important. Let's now turn our attention to where you are you going. Start by asking yourself the honest (and hard) question, *what do I hope to gain by developing my intuition and listening to my inner voice?* When you ask yourself this, don't ponder the question too long or hard. Your inner voice, your intuition does not deliberate. It doesn't need to, it already knows. It's your ego that will cause you to weigh the options and linger over decisions. All your intuition and inner voice require is that you are honest and perhaps even a bit selfish. With that in mind, I ask you again, *what do you desire?*

One may assume this is an easy question to answer. It isn't. Desires are multifaceted, complex and motivated by many factors. As you attempt to answer the question, you may find yourself feeling guilty. You may feel your desires are petty. This may lead you to responses like, *"I want to help people."* If you do, delve deeper. Why? For one, the goal is vague. How do you want to help people? Do you want to care for the sick? Do you want to be a philanthropist? Identify what it is you want to do.

Additionally, when considering your hopes, attempt to identify a "selfish desire." This is your life, after-all. If you feel guilty about not being completely altruistic, don't. Few people are. And consider this, if you aren't pursuing your ambitions, who else will? No one else is as invested in the outcome of your life as you. Further, if your ambition isn't personally motivated, it makes it hard to manifest, for chances are you aren't being honest even with yourself regarding what you want, or you aren't truly committed. Consider Renee. She is an alcoholic who during an intervention orchestrated by her family, complied with her family's request to go into rehabilitation and emphatically agreed she wanted and needed to get clean. She attended rehab and support groups, but then would drink at night as she didn't want to deal with the underlying cause of her excessive drinking. Until she resolves the conflict between her desire to become sober and the desire to avoid her psychological traumas that instigate her drinking, she will not accomplish her goal.

The voices of loved ones, acquaintances, even strangers may reverberate loudly and as Renee demonstrated may not only impact your story but also direct the choices you make and life you lead. Soft, and perhaps overshadowed, there is another voice that is always whispering to you. Your intuition. This voice soothed you as an infant, whispered in your ear at school in an attempt to direct you towards activities in alignment with your life purpose, and nudged you during dates towards compatible matches and away from incompatible ones. Not a day of your life has passed where your life has not been informed by this inner knowing, whether you recognize it or not.

Where the shoves by individuals on the physical plane are loud and perhaps forceful, the nudges from your intuition will often be gentle. Where insight provided by individuals in your life is tainted for good and bad by those individuals' unique perspectives, your intuition is informed by your life purpose and as a result directs you towards your highest and best. Your loved ones and associates may offer you solutions and push you into action, your inner voice rarely will. Rather, your intuition will guide you and simply place opportunities in your path. It becomes your responsibility to take them. Let's liken the guidance your intuition provides to that of kindly parents. These parents may offer financial support to their child allowing him or her to attend college. The child ultimately is responsible for attending classes. Your intuition will present you with opportunities that when seized will lead you to your life purpose. With that in mind, ponder the big question again: *what do you want?* Take a moment to reflect on your desires.

Questions to Consider

Is there a type of situation you continue to find yourself in? If yes, what are the common threads?

Have you found yourself attracted to the same type of individual or organization or activity?

What role did you find yourself playing?

Were there themes that popped up again and again?

Do you find that a desire continues to manifest itself throughout your life?

How would you feel if any of the thoughts you've just pondered were removed from your story? What could you not live without?

As you think about these experiences, consider how they fit into your story. Recognizing the themes that arise again and again in your life offers insight into your life purpose. In my story, mysticism is everywhere and comprises my most profound and vivid memories. These memories are sometimes life-altering as discussed earlier in the book, other times they are experiences that despite being seemingly insignificant, the occurrence sticks in my consciousness. Take for example a memory from college. Due to the accident and the fact it was more than twenty years ago, my memories of college are jumbled and disjointed. Despite that, I vividly recall a moment from the Spring Fest of my freshman year. The college had a number of activities occurring throughout the campus, one being a palm reader. She was set up in the campus center and I recall waiting what felt like hours to see her. To this day, I can recall the feeling of the palm reader's hand touching mine and tracing the lines as she gave me a reading. Just as vivid is the indignation I felt as she informed me my life would be filled with loneliness and disappointment. Another intense memory is a night from my high school days. This particular night, I was woken from a dead sleep to my name being called from within the house. The voice still echoes in my head. Just as clearly, I can picture myself standing at the top of the stairs calling out into the darkened house, *"What do you want?"* as my mother opened her door at the end of the hall to check if I was all right.

Vivid memories like these speak to your soul's purpose. Those memories that are as crystal clear as the day they happened or that immediately transport you back to that moment in time so you can once again see, hear, feel, smell and taste all the sensations, offer a glimpse into your inner desires. These images are a method your inner voice uses to reflect your soul's inner desires and yearnings. Take a moment to reflect on your memories.

> ### Questions to Consider
>
> *What memories are striking?*
>
> *Why are these memories most striking?*
>
> *What insights do they provide regarding your life purpose and your desires?*

Hopefully at this point in the chapter you have a sense of what are some of your deepest desires are. Awareness of your desires is perhaps the most powerful tool you possess in being able to manifest your desires, which leads me to ask again, *what do you want?* Let's now work towards getting it for you.

CHAPTER SEVENTEEN
VISUALIZE YOUR DESIRES

"Our thoughts, our feelings, our dreams, our ideas are physical in the universe. That if we dream something, if we picture something, it adds a physical thrust towards realization that we can put into the universe."
Will Smith

Awareness of your desires is important, but it doesn't mean your hopes and dreams will automatically materialize. For your ambitions to come to fruition, you have work to do. You are, after all, the captain of your own ship and responsible for getting yourself to your ultimate destination.

In getting to your destination, the manifestation of your desires, you have the ability to choose the route you take to get there by filling in the whos, the whats and the hows. As captain of your ship and author of your destiny, you could opt for the fastest and most direct route, or you could take the scenic route with pit stops along the way. That is your choice. It's similar to a road trip my husband I and made to Florida. While planning it, we recognized we had several routes to choose to from. There was the fast course that would get us to our destination in the quickest time. Another route that took longer but would have us pass by family and would give us the opportunity to stop and visit with them along the way was also possible. After weighing the options, we elected to take the fastest route. Perhaps your choice would have been different.

In this example, we CHOSE our travel plan. In your life, you need to CHOOSE your path as well. Many mistakenly believe that through intuition they will be directed down the right path and that their intuition will tell them what actions to take. That is not the case. Your intuition will only provide you with nudges that guide you in the right direction and provide you with tools to assist you in your endeavors. Your inner voice might even intervene if you have strayed from your path in order to redirect you back towards your goals. That voice will never tell you what to do. Why? Because your destiny is not about arriving at a specific destination such as the road trip destination of Florida; rather, it consists of the lessons and experiences you have along the way. Growth and evolution do not occur when someone tells you what to do, rather it occurs when an individual stretches his or her comprehension and his or her comfort zone.

Even though the universe will not simply tell you what to do or give you your desires, it will guide and help you along the way. Your inner voice will provide you with options, much like a parent offering his or her child options for breakfast such as cereal or yogurt. These options are likely presented to the child because the parent knows his or her little one enjoys these foods and may not eat other foods like oatmeal or eggs. Like the parent, if the universe knows what you desire it can more adequately align energies to get you to where you want to be. Unfortunately, if you don't provide clear guidance, the universe will struggle with providing you options. Continuing the parent metaphor, consider the child is a toddler who last week would eat nothing but Cheerios. Hoping for success, the parent offers his or her child a bowl of the cereal. If the toddler has changed his or her mind and has decided he or she no longer likes Cheerios, he or she may freak out leaving the parent scrambling to find an alternative option. The same may be true of you, your dreams and your inner voice's attempt to assist you in the manifestation of your ambitions. If you are not clear or you waffle about your desires, it will be harder for your intuition to provide you with those nudges.

Fortunately, the practice of visualization will assist you in fleshing out your desires. Visualization is a term used to describe any exercise that when applied assists an individual to better communicate and envision a message through the use of imagery. This technique is powerful in the manifestation of one's ambitions as it sharpens the intention of the outcome. Once an outcome is clearly defined, it becomes easier for both you and your intuition to determine strategies or tactics that can assist you in accomplishing said goal. For example, when my husband and I were house hunting, while we had a list of must haves, the list kept changing. One day my husband would insist on a whirlpool tub, and the next the tub was out but a particular neighborhood was in. As we vacillated over our list of desires, so did the type of homes that were presented to us by both our relator and the universe. The day my husband insisted on a whirlpool tub, we drove by a house that peaked our interest and coincidently (or not) on of the features of the house was a whirlpool tub, whereas when the neighborhood became our priority, a new house came on the market in the desired location. It wasn't until we narrowed our focus that the universe was able to do the same and provide us with more ideal options from which to choose. That is why honing your desires is of vital importance.

To accomplish that laser vision, there is a variety of visualization techniques to apply. One technique is meditation, another is the creation of a vision board, and a third is goal setting. These practices can be used singularly or as a unit. No matter how you choose to apply them, the act of working through the exercise will assist you in seeing concrete steps that will inch you towards your ultimate goal.

Let's start with a discussion of meditation. Partaking in quiet reflection to visualize your goals is a beneficial activity. Through meditation, more than the creation of a vision board or strategic plan, you have the ability to connect with your inner voice and your purpose. In doing so, those quiet whispers are directing you as opposed to your ego. This is powerful in that it is not uncommon if the ego is speaking for individuals to place an emphasis on the means of obtaining the goal, as opposed to the goal itself. For example, if an individual is creating a vision board, he or she may focus on elements of the home he or she desires such as the size and layout of the kitchen, rather than the underlying motivation, which may be the desire to have a space where family and friends can gather. Is the difference of perspective bad? No. But it means an individual may be missing one's true motivations and intent and as a result miss options that may be a better fit because they are unaware of them.

To conduct a visualization, you are encouraged to find a comfortable and quiet location. If you find it relaxing, dim the lights, light a candle and/or turn on comforting music. Once you have created a peaceful environment, close your eyes and focus on your desires. Allow your thoughts and imagination to flow. Envision your life after accomplishing your desired goal. Vividly picture yourself at a future time and location. In your mind's eye, see the environment of the chosen time. Picture how you have aged and the comforts that surround you. Hear with your ears the words from yourself, others and your environment. Breathe in the smells. Feel with your heart the happiness you have accomplished. Complete this visualization.

> ### Questions to Consider
>
> *Why does accomplishing my goal make me happy?*
>
> *How has my life changed since I accomplished this goal?*
>
> *What actions did I take that assisted me in achieving my ambition?*
>
> *What advice do you have for yourself to assist you in accomplishing these goals?*
>
> *What elements of the glorious future are takeaways you can focus on as motivations?*

The time meditating on your goals is time well spent, however, it is not the most effective visualization technique. Meditation, while it provides inspiration and insight, often lacks tangible and actionable steps. You may find yourself inspired by the vision and wish to await the amazing outcomes. Unfortunately, if you do not take action on the images that flooded your meditation, those goals will remain in the realm of dreams and are unlikely to come to fruition. For example, Rebecca deeply desired a romantic partner. She would complete visualization meditations in an effort to attract the man of her dreams. Beyond that, she took few steps towards bringing that man into her life. She didn't join a dating website and she rarely went out. When she did go out, it was always with friends and she limited her interactions to those individuals. No steps were taken. As a result, she continued to dream.

Remaining in the realm of dreams is the potential limitation of meditation as a visualization technique. To negate this shortcoming, one can elect to create a vision board. A vision board is a visual representation of one's desires. As individuals carefully select images, words and phrase, they solidify both for themselves and the universe their intended outcomes. Crafting a vision board is beneficial because upon the completion of a vision board, you have a tangible piece of art that if strategically placed in a position that you observe frequently, it will serve as a visual reminder of your hopes and dreams and could provide you with accountability. As an added benefit, it also provides you with a physical representation of the potential manifestation of your desire. For example, Cindy created a vision board when she was looking to purchase a new house. She cut out images of living, dining and bathrooms. Upon walking into the home she ended up purchasing, she instantly knew it was the one because the house contained many elements featured on her board.

The creation of a vision board is fun and easy. To create a vision board first collect the following items: a heavy duty piece of paper or canvas, scissors, glue, magazines and writing utensils such as markers and pens. Once you have collected all these materials, consider what it is you wish to manifest. With that in mind, flip through magazines to find visual representations of those goals. If you are unable to find visual representations within the periodicals, go to a computer and search for images. If you find a picture you like, print it out. After collecting a variety of pictures, arrange them on the paper or canvas and glue them down. Be creative. It is important that you remember, the vision board is a work in progress, you have the ability to add and subtract items at your discretion.

A vision board is a powerful tool, much like meditation. But like meditation, it also has its inadequacies. Similar to meditation, it does not provide you with action steps. As a result, while you are reminded of your desires and that unconsciously drives you towards their manifestation, it does not give you strategies to complete those tasks. Additionally, as this serves as a visual representation it may place a focus on the materialistic side of your ambitions as opposed to your life purpose. Be careful not to view the accomplishment of the physical as the soul manifestation of your goals.

The final visualization technique to be discussed within this book is goal-setting. This technique is powerful in that it resolves the shortcoming of lack of specific action steps. Goal setting and the creation of specific strategies, activities and tactics provide you with a route to follow towards your destination. This is often accomplished by defining short, intermediate and long-term goals. Consider the example of my husband and my road trip to Florida used earlier in this chapter. Once we reviewed the potential routes and selected the one that best suited our needs, we were able to start hashing out the details of that trip. The map indicated the trip, in total, would take about twenty hours. With this in mind we strategically considered how many days that drive would be stretched over, what time we would leave in an effort to avoid traffic and to minimize the discomfort to our daughter, and where we would stop along the way. After looking at our options, we realized that much was dependent on where we would be stopping as there were stretches in our journey with few amenities. With this in mind, we were able to chart a path that was uneventful and as enjoyable as twenty plus hours in a car can be.

While the road trip may be trivial in the grand scheme, the tactics employed are no different than those you should employ as your work towards attaining your life purpose. To achieve your aspirations, you should start by reviewing the potential pathways you could take. Once you've done that and chosen your route, you then should entertain all of the factors that will impact your goals. In business they call this a SWOT analysis where you identify your strengths, your weakness, opportunities and potential threats. These steps are ones you may have accomplished if you took the time to meditate and/or create a vision board. Goal setting will take you the next step as you develop short, intermediate and long-term goals. Let's get started on that now.

As you reflect on your ambitions, I encourage you to create SMART goals which are **S**pecific, **M**easurable, **A**ttainable, **R**ealistic and **T**ime sensitive. This approach is utilized by businesses in their strategic and goal planning pursuits. Surprisingly, individuals, even those trained in this modality, rarely utilize the tool in their own lives. Despite its lack of use, it is relevant, powerful, and the creation of SMART goals will bring you closer to your targets.

To start the process of setting SMART goals, consider your desire and meditate on it. Your aspiration may be like mine to normalize mediumship and intuition or you may wish to live comfortably in financial security. Whatever the goal, define what that looks like and ask yourself specific questions. For example, if you strive for financial security, how will you know you have achieved that security? Will you have paid off your debt? Or will that success be measured by having a rainy-day fund? If the buffer is what you seek, how much would you ideally like to have saved? Is it a thousand dollars? Ten thousand? A hundred thousand? Or a million? The specifics are important because they provide a threshold and indicate when you have accomplished the goal. Without it, even though you may have a million dollars in your account you may not feel the financial security and instead find yourself continuing to seek more.

More important than the specifics of the goal, such as paying off debt or having a rainy-day fund, you should also ensure you realize why that goal is important to you. In order to determine this, you may need to reflect on your story. For example, while considering the purchase of a home a few locations were attractive. Each had amenities such as a grocery store, gas store, medical facilities within walking distance. Further, each was known for the friendliness of its neighbors and the strong community. Upon reflection, I realized these aspects were important to me because I don't drive. If a tragedy were to limit my husband's ability to drive, even for a couple of days, I wanted the security of knowing we would be okay. The proximity of fundamental amenities assured that and the perception that I would have a community to depend on reinforced that belief. The realization of my unconscious motivations was helpful as it allowed my husband and me to further zero in on where to purchase a house as the proximity to a bus line was added to our list of must-haves. By understanding the underlying motivations, we were able to manifest our desire. You will be able to do the same. Take a moment to reflect on the following question: *What is it that you specifically wish to manifest in your life?*

Identifying the specific nature of the goal goes hand in hand with the creation of a measure of success. As mentioned in the previous paragraphs, having a measure of success allows you to recognize when you have reached your target. For example, rather than wishing to *"be rich,"* instead you state, *"I will have a million dollars in my savings account."* Being rich is subjective, a million dollars is not. Determining that measure can be tricky, especially when you consider an aspiration like mine of normalizing mediumship and intuition. How does one measure that?

To identify measures for more subjective and obscure goals, place a focus not on the end goal but rather on the steps you can take to get you there. For example, a short-term goal of mine is to speak on intuition to groups in at least twelve events. The twelve events are the goal that is measurable. Will this ensure that mediumship and intuition are normalized? No. But the action brings me one step closer since during those speaking engagements I have the opportunity to reach people and spread my message. At this time, I encourage you to reflect on your specific goal and identify measures you can utilize that will bring you closer to your aspirations. While doing that, consider the following question: *What measures will demonstrate that I am progressing towards my goal?*

Once a specific goal is identified and measures are determined, two tough questions need to be asked: *is my vision attainable?* And, *is it realistic?* Let's start with the question of attainability. Your desires are attainable. However, this is only true if you adhered to the guidance offered previously and made the goal selfish. Goals are only attainable if YOU have control over the outcome. Your objectives are not attainable if you are reliant on someone else. As the Genie said in Aladdin, *"I can't make anyone fall in love with anyone else";* a wish or desire that changes someone else's beliefs or circumstances is outside of your control. For example, imagine your goal is to manage your diabetic husband's health by lowering his A1C level. This goal is specific and measurable, but it may be unattainable goal. Why? It's not because it's impossible for him to lower his A1C level. Rather, it is unattainable because you have no control over whether that goals is attained or not. You could monitor his diet and allow for only healthy foods in the house, but he may choose to stop by the gas station every time he is out to purchase candy bars and slushies which would negate your efforts. As a result, the status of his health is his goal. Similarly, this makes my goal of normalizing mediumship unattainable. I know that. I know my role will be a small one, and I am satisfied with the small impact I may have.

With that in mind, I encourage you to reflect on your aspirations. If you discover your ambitions are not attainable because they are outside your control, do not be discouraged. More importantly, do not abandon your ambition. Rather, reflect on the goal and consider the aspects you DO have control of. For example, by speaking at twelve venues, I am aware that provides me with the opportunity to touch lives in each location. Even if I only speak to two people at each location and only one of them walks away with insight, I'm influencing twelve people. Those twelve people go out in the world and influence an indeterminant number of individuals. The message is being spread, even if I can't see it. That's ok with me. As you consider this, reflect on the following: *I may not see my goal come to fruition, am I okay with that? What do I need to see to be happy? And, how do I make my goal attainable?*

Just as any goal is attainable, all goals are realistic. Your aspirations, however, are only realistic if you WORK towards them. For example, you can save a million dollars. Depending on where you are in your life, this may feel impossible. It isn't. The only time it's unrealistic is when you create circumstances that contradict your aspiration. Take Duke as an example. He is a hard worker with a relatively good job, but he is constantly struggling to financially get ahead in life. His financial difficulties are a result of several life choices. One, rather than pursuing college or vocational education, he took a job at a local factory and throughout his career he has elected not to pursue any specialized or managerial training. While he could be doing better, the factory provides him with livable income. The comfort those wages provide is limited as Duke has six kids between two ex-wives. The child support and alimony he pays he views as crippling. Should he review the finances, he'd recognize that his life could have more comforts if these were the only expenses he had. The next actions that make a goal of saving money appear unrealistic are the following habits: He smokes two packs of cigarettes a day. At more than ten dollars a pack, that is more than $7,000 a year. Additionally, he spends an exorbitant amount of money on gifts for the kids. For the holidays, he routinely spends two to five thousand dollars on each child. If you quickly add that up, that could easily be an extra $12,000 in his pocket each year. Rather than seeing the places money could be saved, he viewed he goal as unrealistic. Perhaps you feel the same way. If you do, you are encouraged to explore why you feel it's unrealistic and identify ways you could accomplish your goal. You are not stuck, you just need to change the way you view things and perhaps break the goal down to a more manageable target. Instead of aiming for a million dollars, strive for ten thousand. At this point, reflect on the following question: *Is my goal realistic? If not, how can it become realistic?*

Finally, it is important that your goals are time sensitive. Don't say "someday." If you do, someday will never come. It is like my husband, if I tell him we are running low on toilet paper, he may or may not remember to pick some up when he is at the store. Without a measure of reference, the toilet paper we have may last a day or it may last three weeks, but if I tell him we are down to our last roll, chances are before I finish the sentence, he is putting on his shoes to go to the store and buy some. A time frame provides a sense of urgency, even if that sense of need occurs at a future date.

As you determine time frames, be aware that even the best laid plans are sometimes delayed, and that timing can be outside of your control. The fluidity of timing is one of the biggest frustrations my students have. They will receive nudges and those that follow those inklings to no resolve become confused and frustrated. Take my client Ken. He received the message that a job was coming soon. He pulled together his resume, networked with his friends, but two years later still no job. Then it came, it was what the inner voice had been pushing him toward.

I wish I had divine guidance, but unfortunately I do not, other than to say, trust that the universe has a reason and everything happens in its divine time. Perhaps Ken had a lesson to learn through the process. Perhaps had he taken a job, it wouldn't have brought him to where he was meant to be. The universe is fluid and ever changing. As a result, view time frames more like guideposts than deadlines. Let's take a moment to place a time frames on your goals. Consider the following: *When do I want to accomplish my goal by?*

Having elaborated on your goals, here is some advice. Be flexible. Know that it is probable your goals will not manifest in the designated time and that they may not manifest themselves in the way you imagined. Take for example Nanette, a student and dear friend. Nanette and I had been working to get her in touch with her intuition, mediumship abilities and guides. After a number of disappointments, Nanette was frustrated and feeling let down by her guides. I informed her that I believed it was good to be frustrated and encouraged her to ask the universe to demonstrate they are listening and more importantly working to bring her hopes and dreams to life.

Nanette is a dutiful student and she took my recommendation to heart. After pondering it, she put the following request to the universe: *"My birthday is in a few weeks and Josh Groban is putting on a show in a town an hour away on my special day. I want tickets, good seats and a ride to the show."*

This was an excellent goal as it was specific and measurable: tickets to the concert. It was also attainable because while someone could purchase tickets for her, she could purchase them for herself. The goal was realistic because tickets were still available and not ridiculously priced. And it was time sensitive, the concert happened on her birthday in only a few weeks.

A week after her birthday, I met with Nanette and was curious as to the outcome. She was in a funk and even angrier than she was the last time we met. She recounted that it was the worst birthday she'd ever had and that more than anything she was disappointed her goal hadn't been manifested. I kept hearing the universe whisper, *"We tried."* I kept my mouth shut knowing that without clarity around the situation, me saying *"they tried"* was not going to help. Fortunately, as she continued to vent, I was provided with the information I needed to demonstrate the opportunity was indeed present. Nanette shared that while her birthday was dreadful, there was a moment of pure excitement. She shared that lifelong friend had sent two pieces of mail: one was a birthday card and the other was an unexpected note. When Nanette opened the letter, she was flabbergasted when she found it contained a check worth a thousand dollars with her friend simply stating, *"do something special for yourself!"*

Upon hearing that, I responded, *"Nanette, they provided you with the money to go."* She retorted, *"Well I didn't get the check until the afternoon of my birthday, by that point it was too late."* My intuition told me she was mistaken and upon query, she revealed the cards had arrived a week earlier and she had saved them for her birthday. Had she opened the cards upon receipt and noted that this money could have been spent on the tickets, her wish could have manifested itself. Lesson in this, look at all the potential ways your dreams can come to fruition.

In addition to looking for the variety of ways your goal is manifesting, be flexible and know it is okay to modify your goals. Just like you should not and do not remain stagnant, neither should your goals. Just as you are evolving your goals will as well. You can and they should. Knowing this, I reevaluate my goals every single year. While friends are making New Year's resolutions, I am recommitting and modifying my goals to be in alignment with who I am today. I encourage you to do the same. If you do, you will be amazed as it is likely that the targets you reach are better than expected.

CHAPTER EIGHTEEN
BELIEVE IT'S POSSIBLE

"I am the greatest. I said that even before I knew I was."
Muhammad Ali

You will likely be motivated by the beautiful imagery you saw while you meditate and featured on your vision board. You are also likely inspired to take action knowing that the goals you identified are within your reach. It is important to note, visualizing your desires will only takes you so far. Not only do you have to take action and actively pursue those desires, it is imperative that you BELIEVE your desires are possible and that you deserve the abundance that will be received upon the realization of those goals. If you do not have faith in those two beliefs, you will likely find yourself met with challenges and your desires will remain just out of reach.

Consider Madison. She is a talented physician with a thriving practice. Over the past few years she has undergone a personal evolution and experienced spiritual growth. As a result, she wishes to incorporate new modalities into her practice. She has done the research and created a plan outlining the incorporation of the new techniques, but she is terrified. She hears her husband telling her she's *"crazy"* to consider it. The insurance companies have indicated that the change in course may affect her reimbursement rates. Her clients have provided her with neutral feedback. Most significantly, the response from her husband, the insurance companies and clients reinforce her belief that she is less than worthy. As a result, despite all her planning, her dream doesn't manifest. She doesn't believe it can.

You may be like Madison. Despite painting a beautiful picture, you may doubt whether these goals are possible or perhaps whether you deserve them. Fortunately, restructuring your belief system through awareness of your story and cognitive reframing techniques can assist you in liberating you from the limiting mindsets. This is why you were encouraged to reflect on your experiences. If you understand where you came from and more importantly the belief system you operate within, you will more easily be able to recognize the beliefs that are working against you. You can then focus your efforts towards reframing those specific beliefs. Think of it in terms of medicine. If you go to the doctor complaining of a headache, the doctor can prescribe a medication to alleviate the pain. While this treatment manages the symptom and will be successful in managing acute situations such as a headache resulting from a bump to the head, if the headache is a result of a chronic condition (like your deeply ingrained belief systems) the pain medication will only serve as a short-term solution. Because an underlying cause exists that hasn't been addressed, while the pain medication may alleviate pain today, the headache is likely to recur. In order to address a chronic condition (the stories you tell yourself), a healthcare provider delves deeper into the root cause (introspection into your story). In terms of the headache, the provider will ask questions and through that inquiry discover that the headache occurs every time foods containing nitrites such as pepperoni and salami are ingested. In compliance with the doctor's recommendation, the patient may subsequently avoid problematic foods and as a result the frequency of headaches decreases. By addressing the cause, not the symptom, a long-term solution has been developed. Similarly, when you uncover the roots of your belief systems, you can release that belief and formulate one that serves you better. In most instances, the belief system that serves you better already exists. It exists because your inner voice knows your unique and individual path to happiness. Fortunately, recognition and awareness of the unhealthy thought patterns is usually enough to free yourself from its influence.

Sound amazing? It is! And fortunately, cognitive reframing does not require monumental change; rather, it is accomplished by making small modifications to your behaviors every day. As mentioned, the first step is knowing your story. Once you know your story, you can identify opportunities for change. Those limitations may be the times you hear yourself parroting others' opinions or where fear and lack of confidence inhabit your actions. After identifying those opportunities, the next step is to carefully choose the language you employ. Place a focus on what you desire and wish to bring into your life instead of commenting on what you feel is lacking. For example, if an individual is concerned about his or her finances, he or she would be encouraged to avoid saying, *"I don't know if I'll be able to afford that upcoming trip"* and instead remark, *"The upcoming trip is going to be worth every penny."* To put it simply, instead of saying *"I can't,"* focus on what you *"can."* Consider this, as you know I am unable to drive. Instead of focusing on the significant restrictions this could create in my life, I do not allow myself to feel limited. I know I can take the bus, lean on my husband, call a friend, and with ride shares now available in my area, I can utilize rides share as well. While my inability to drive does not impact me negatively, it does have a detrimental effect on my husband. Of my solutions mentioned, he is the resource I use most frequently. Aware that I am reliant on him, he has adopted the belief that he must be available should I need a ride. Due to his belief, he feels he *can't* apply for a traditional nine-to-five job and he *can't* spend too long with friends, for both would take him from the home and my daughter or I *might* need him while he's out. Because of this belief he feels confined, has difficulty identifying goals and without goals, he struggles with obtaining happiness. Reframing his thoughts and words would benefit him greatly as he might recognize the limitations he places on himself.

Unfortunately, as I know from the example just referenced regarding my husband, breaking the cycle of detrimental thought patterns is easier said than done. An individual has a lifetime of experiences, good and bad, to overcome. For example, throughout his life my husband has felt as though he has let people down. Having felt the retribution after letting individuals down before, he is driven to not allow this to occur again, which results in his desire to always be available for my daughter and myself. If your experience is like my husband where it has demonstrated hardship, you could alter your words, but you may not really believe them.

Take George for example. Ten years ago, he and his wife divorced. Since then, he has sought a healthy and loving relationship. Unfortunately, he has had little success. While ruminating over this, in one breath he says, *"I'm a catch"* and in the next *"I hate looking in the mirror for all I see is an old man."* His words are conflicted and a representation of the turmoil that occurs within. You may experience the same thing. I know I do. Unfortunately, when one is conflicted the negative or unhealthy belief often overshadows the good and your intuition.

If you struggle with reframing your vocabulary and find an undesirable mindset prevails, start by not by focusing on the places you know you lack confidence, rather identify places where you hear others speaking for you. For example, if you find yourself saying, *"Oh my goodness, I sound just like my mother!"* and you don't view this positively, that an excellent starting place. Or, if you find yourself repeating gossip. Again, another great place to begin. How do you begin? If you find yourself making a comment you don't really believe or you realize that your words mimic those of another, take a moment to pause and reflect on the following: *Do I truly believe what I am saying?* If you do, don't change a thing. At least not yet. If you don't, stop yourself and modify your thoughts and words to be in alignment with what you do believe. This may be challenging as you may find you contradict yourself. Do not be embarrassed if this is the case. You are allowed to change. You are permitted to be yourself. Let your inner voice speak.

Another place to start is replacing the word *"try"* with *"will"* or *"no."* If you are like me, you reply *"I'll try"* when you aren't sure you are capable of or don't want to perform a particular feat. For example, my colleague Susie used to invite me to a gathering every month. At first, I would reply, *"I'll try,"* but when I was honest with myself, I had no intention of going. Finally, I was truthful with her and responded, *"I'd love to, but it is my day off and I want to spend time with my daughter."* After revealing that, a huge weight was lifted and I no longer felt guilty for spending the time with my family. Similarly, I changed my language while writing this book. I would comment, *"I'm going to try to write today."* On those days, I didn't write. When I changed my language to, *"I'm going to write today,"* I did. Changing my verbiage in these two places not only allowed me to accomplish my tasks, it also made me happier. You will likely find the same thing.

A third place to focus on modifying your language is to take the phrase *"I'm sorry"* out of your vocabulary. In today's society, we overuse and often misuse this phrase. When this phrase is utilized, it often unconsciously transfers a portion of responsibility onto the speaker's shoulders. This is asinine, especially since the phrase is often utilized when the speaker has no responsibility at all, like when an individual says to his or her friend who has lost a loved one, *"I'm sorry for your loss."* The individual may sympathize or empathize with his or her friend and wish to express condolences, but he or she does not need to say, *"I'm sorry."* By removing it from your vocabulary, you will find that the empathy you feel will be released in a more prompt fashion.

These three vocabulary places are a great place to begin. Think they sound easy? They aren't. Every day you will need to be vigilant and consciously aware of your words and thoughts. It is a lot of work and is sometimes exhausting. But skipping the step of cognitive reframing is ill-advised, and you may be tempted.

Why might you want to skip this step? And what might happen if you do? You may wish to skip this step because you don't want to focus on the past. You may believe that by focusing on the past it is inhibiting your ability to move forward. If this is your assertion, you do make a valid point. Living in the past, be it by idolizing it or seeing yourself as the victim or martyr, is counterproductive. But not recognizing the past's influence on today is a disservice to yourself as well. Knowing your history is important because it offers an explanation as to why you may behave in a certain manner. For example, I know that the frustration I feel towards my husband at seeing a sink full of dirty dishes at the end of a work day harkens back to the arguments I overheard my parents have over the same situation when I was a child. Knowing that, while it doesn't erase the frustration, it minimizes it as I no longer allow the past to influence the present. Delving through your past is important and recommended; just be careful and avoid the pitfalls which include agonizing over the past. Instead recognize the factors, understand why they bother you and then move on.

You may also be tempted to skip this pivotal step because you want change and you want it NOW. Unfortunately, the process of self-discovery is both time-consuming and tedious. Because lessons learned during this process are complex and multi-faceted, an individual may find him or herself going back to a situation multiple times before full awareness occurs. For example, Henry struggles with change, especially when it comes to his home. During any home renovation, his anxiety goes through the roof. To understand this better, he searched for answers and determined that it was due to his upbringing. His father was a contractor and as a result chose to save the family money by completing tasks himself. Unfortunately, his father had a tendency of starting projects but never finished them. As a result, Henry's home was often in a torn-up state. He thought this was the root of his anxiety. When his stress did not diminish upon that realization, he delved deeper. Upon doing so, he recognized that the root of his anxiety went back further in his childhood. He recalled being dropped off for long durations of time, sometimes a few days and sometimes a few months. During these periods of time, he'd have no contact with his parents and no idea when (or if) they would return. When they did eventually reenter his life and he returned home, he always noticed changes occurred such as new paint or furniture. Henry associated the changes in the home with the discord he felt as a young boy. Upon recognizing that, the anxiety lessened and he now has an easier time with home renovations. Had he not been introspective, he would have been unable to reframe his beliefs.

Still others avoid this step because it is uncomfortable. When an individual explores aspects of him or herself, he or she may be uncovering ugly truths about him or herself which may cause the individual to be ashamed, embarrassed or feel guilty. As I review my own past, there are multiple instances when I reflect where I am astounded by my behavior and guilt steeps in. An example, I was in high school and a group of friends and I decided to go to the beach and sunbathe. While there we witnessed a flamboyant man in a bright orange speedo and neon yellow fishnet top. My friends and I giggled and cat-called the man. I was embarrassed then, I am more embarrassed today. In those moments it is important to not beat yourself up. Instead recognize how much you have grown; the guilt and shame evidence that. And it reinforces the growth as you will likely be more cognizant not to repeat the behavior in the future.

Finally, some avoid this step because of the backlash they receive from their loved ones, colleagues, peers and even acquaintances. Why? The changes you are undergoing will not only impact you and your internal story, they affect your interactions with others. While you may want to change, others may not want you to. In fact, these individuals are likely the people who influenced you to begin with. To dissuade you from changing, these individuals may respond with aggression. Take Ella for example. Ella is married to Gus. She has always maintained the household by doing laundry, paying bills and ensuring a warm meal is on the table every night. Over the years, Ella has felt as though she's lost her identity. To remedy that, she obtained a part-time job which caused her to be unable to prepare dinner two nights during the week. This change has upset Gus, who insisted that Ella quit her job. Loving the new job, Ella found herself torn. If you have ever attempted to grow, you have likely found yourself in a similar situation.

Despite the attraction of skipping the step of demonstrating to yourself that you are worthy of your aspirations, don't. If you don't truly believe you deserve the outcome, it won't manifest. It also won't manifest if you find yourself conflicted, even subconsciously, over the desired outcome. Consider the following: an individual wants to move out of state as job opportunities are limited, and the weather negatively impacts his or her health. Simultaneously, that individual values the close relationships he or she has with his or her family and cannot imagine being away from them. If this is the case, the individual's dream of moving out of state will be hindered by his or her love of family. As a result, it is likely that every time he or she takes one step forward towards the move, he or she will simultaneously take one step back. If the conflict is not recognized, it is unlikely a move will occur, and the individual will remain in a constant state of limbo. However, if the individual has awareness of the conflict, while a move may or may not occur, the individual will be making a conscious choice as an active participant in his or her life as opposed to remaining in the uncomfortable limbo. Your awareness will allow your inner voice or intuition to speak and shine a light upon that which compliments your life purpose. Without awareness, you will remain a prisoner to your past and your current circumstances, no matter how loudly your inner voice is urging you to change. Fortunately, simply by being aware of your past and consciously choosing your words and thoughts, action will follow. Be aware of this: you do not take a battering ram to your belief system, rather you dismantle it brick by brick. Then using those same bricks, you brick by brick refashion your belief system into one of your choosing. Change will occur through those small steps.

CHAPTER NINETEEN
DEUX IT

"Go confidently in the direction of your dreams. Live the life you have imagined."
Henry David Thoreau

It is time to ask yourself hard questions: *Am I ready to do the hard work, stop making excuses for myself and be happy?* and *Am I ready to listen to my inner voice, no matter what discoveries that leads me to?* If you are not, that is okay. It might not be the right time and you have every day of your life to change your mind. If you are, CONGRATULATIONS! You are taking a huge step. You are about to find yourself on an amazing journey to your intuition, which you will soon find isn't about what you *hear*, it's about what you *know*. More importantly, it is about how you live. It is about living in harmony with the universe, but more than that it's about being one with your soul which will bring you an indescribable peace.

Living in harmony with your soul, while it will bring you peace and joy, isn't easy. There will be people who don't like you. In fact, there will be people who downright hate you as you will challenge their belief systems. These individuals may even work to undermine you and your beliefs every chance they get. Not only that, you will carry with you a feeling of social responsibility the likes of which you have never felt before. You will no longer be able to avoid personal responsibility and consider challenges as personal assaults; rather, you will own your actions and recognize how they lead to both the desirable and undesirable outcomes in your life. As you no longer find yourself blaming others, you will hold yourself to a higher standard. This is an uncomfortable place to be and takes some getting used to. As with any transition, it can be bumpy. Consider Anna. She has long been on her path to spirituality and is a gifted medium. In the past few years, she has chosen to embrace her gifts and has begun practicing mediumship professionally. This has caused her challenges in her marriage as she can no longer accept her husband's drinking and depression, for she realizes it is significantly impacting her and her children. With this realization, she has decided to walk away from her marriage of almost twenty years and the security he, as the breadwinner, has afforded. Despite the discomfort, her emotional and spiritual wellbeing are more important. Would you have the courage to do the same thing?

While I pray you would have the courage, I also pray are not presented with the same tough decision. Still, it is likely you will come to a place where your new standards are challenged and you are forced to stand upon your moral pedestal. For Anna it was the relationship with her husband, for me it was the job under the tyrannical boss, Andrea. Because it is likely, perhaps even guaranteed, that you will be faced with tough decisions, before we go any further, take a moment to reflect.

Questions to Consider

What do you hope to gain from listening to your inner voice?

> *What would a life of purpose look like to you?*
>
> *What do you feel like you are lacking? What would you like more of?*
>
> *What values are you unwilling to compromise?*
>
> *What are you willing to sacrifice?*

As you ask yourself these questions, be honest with yourself as well as realistic. Realize that as you pursue your intuition and your dreams, you are going to be faced with a lot of hard work and you are going to need to know what is important to you. The universe is not going to miraculously provide you with all your hopes and dreams, nor is it going to hold your hand and walk you through what to do every step of the way. It doesn't and shouldn't work like that. Let's liken the universe and your inner voice to a coach and you an aspiring athlete. If you yearn to be an Olympian, you must be dedicated to your sport. This dedication requires hours and years of hard work. The Olympian trains in good health, while sick and even with injuries. The Olympian trains when he or she wants to be there, but also when he or she wants to be somewhere else such as the funeral of a loved one or at a school dance. The coach does not force the athlete to show up; that's not the coach's job; rather, the trainer is present when the athlete shows up.

If you wish to live a life of joy in alignment with your life purpose, you have to show up. Not only that, you have to be dedicated and committed because you will have a lot of work to tackle. And I do mean A LOT. Fortunately, that work is almost always rewarding. For example, a friend once commented, *"Dawn, do you realize you have the life people dream of."* He was referencing the flexibility my job affords when it comes to being engaged in my daughter's life and travel, as well as being blessed in regard to loving what I do. I am very fortunate. Ironically, this same friend mentioned a couple months later, *"You are always working, how the heck do you do it?"* I am always working. I always have an iron in the fire as I refuse to become complacent. If I become too comfortable, I find I become lazy and do not actively pick away at my goals. You may witness the same thing in your life. That is why it is necessary to commit to the hard work and be vigilant if you want to break free of your current paradigm and accomplish your goals.

In addition to the hard work, as already referenced, you may have to sacrifice. As you work towards your aspirations, there will be components of your life that you have to give up. If the goal is worthwhile, it won't matter. For example, Rosie's doctor advised her that she should give up her evening glass of red wine to further her goal of losing weight. Rosie loves red wine and she finds not only the medicinal aspects of the wine to be relaxing, but also the habit of drinking the glass brings her quiet time. Her desire for weight loss overshadowed her love of wine, and as a result she sacrificed the wine for her goal. When she did, she immediately experienced additional weight loss. Like Rosie, you may sacrifice, but as you obtain your goals, you will likely find it was worth it.

One of those places you may find you have to sacrifice is with loved ones. A great example of this is my friend Darlene. We used to do EVERYTHING together. We would laugh and joke about how we must have had past lives together and imagined what those past lives looked. She taught me a lot about myself. Gave me confidence to grow as a medium. As I grew, she grew in a different direction. It became harder and harder to be around her as the path she chose and the people she surrounded herself with no longer resonated with the path I was on. And then she began letting me down. I held on tight, until I could hold on no longer and the relationship didn't just fizzle, it imploded. Not because we didn't love the other, but because the lessons we had for one another had been learned. By staying in the relationship, trying desperately to keep things the way they had been was stifling the other's growth. It was time to move on.

Are you beginning to doubt your commitment to pursuing your life purpose? Does the hard work, sacrifice and loss feel like it might be too great? I promise you it isn't. When you are in alignment with your inner voice and your purpose, you will feel as though you are on cloud nine. While the universe may not tell you what to do, you while find yourself surrounded by signs indicating that you are heading in the right direction. For example, while writing this book I was questioned whether the content of this book was relevant or not. To distract myself from the question, I decided to go shopping. As I found myself flipping through a t-shirt rack, I was drawn to a lovely blue shirt, so I pulled it out to examine it further. Upon it I found the following phrase inscribed: *"Write Your Story."* Sign? I think so! It was exactly what I needed in that moment to know I was on the right path. It wasn't the universe telling me what to do. It just provided me with the *"atta girl"* I needed.

As you pursue your ambitions, you will likely get affirmations along the way. If you struggle to see them, which you might because while connecting to your inner voice is easy, recognizing it can prove challenging. I encourage you to BE PERSISTENT. Persistence is a virtue that is invaluable when it comes to manifesting your desires and life purpose. If you keep working towards an end, even if you don't accomplish the goal you had in mind, you will accomplish something. For example, Monica had a good job at a tech company. She loved the organization and found the job engaging. In the infancy of her career, she desired professional growth both for the title and salary that came with it. After conversations with management at her company, it was made clear that it would be unlikely to achieve her goals. Regretfully, she searched and found a new job. The new position offered more pay, but she was unhappy with the environment. Back to the drawing board. She was offered another new job which came with another salary increase and more hassles. She was frustrated and regretted her decision of leaving the job she loved, for no other job compared. Monica was also persistent, she knew that her dream job with the salary she felt she deserved in a healthy environment had to exist. She continued learning, consistently attending seminars and bolstering her resume. About three years after leaving the tech company she loved, the company had a job opening and Monica was contacted to interview for it, and she ultimately was rehired for a job with the responsibilities and pay she desired. She kept working towards her goal, and her hard work paid off.

Throughout the process, Monica was discouraged. You may find yourself discouraged with the process as well, but if you are persistent you will find your hard work pays off. It may be in a week, a month, a year, a decade; the time frame may feel never-ending, but persistence always pays off.

Along with being persistent, I encourage you to HAVE FAITH. Trust that no matter what the situation, good will come of it. I know in the darkest of hours this is hard. Following the car accident, the future seemed bleak and I truly believed no good could come. It did, but only after I believed it could.

If you are in the darkest of hours, these are the tools that assisted me in finding faith: 1) Connect with the universe through prayer and meditation as it provides unparalleled peace and comfort; 2) Surround yourself with laughter, be it your own or another's, as it brings joy, even if it is short-lived, due to a biochemical response within the body; 3) Surround yourself with music as the melodies, words and vibrations will hit you on an emotional, intellectual and spiritual level; and, 4) Go out in nature. These are some of the activities that worked for me, as they helped me see the good in the world; there may be other activities for you.

The final tip I will provide you with, is YOU DEUX YOU. It is not uncommon for an individual to sacrifice happiness and enjoyment for the benefit of another. In doing this, the individual is not honoring his or her needs and/or desires. Take Tina for example. She is a chiropractor and massage therapist. One day while I was in a pinch I sent her a note to see if she had any availability left. It was late in the day, so I was aware that my chances were slim, but I thought I would try anyway. At first she responded, *"I'm actually done for the day."* I responded letting her know I understood and then about ten minutes later she sent another text asking when I would be in the area and that she might be able to arrange to get back to her office. Upon seeing that, I vehemently responded, *"Absolutely not! You are off. I'm going to respect your space even if you don't."* She laughed and the next time I saw her she thanked me. Tina knew it was a lesson she needed to be reminded of. It is a lesson we all have to be reminded of.

When you agree to partake in an activity, regardless of how seemingly trivial, you take the risk of it interfering with one of your aspirations. That is why it is imperative that you are committed and invested in everything you do. If you practice discretion in your activities, you will find you garner enjoyment from almost every moment. And if not enjoyment, at the very least you won't feel torn because you will know you made the conscious decision to participate in the activity.

If you follow these recommendations, your ambitions and your life purpose will begin to manifest. Additionally, you will notice that you are being guided by your internal compass of intuition, without any effort on your part. Your inner voice may not speak with a booming voice; rather, you'll find that you feel compelled to do what your morals deem right.

CHAPTER TWENTY
LIVE PURPOSEFULLY

"People who use time wisely spend it on activities that advance their overall purpose in life."
John C Maxwell

Once you commit to actively pursuing your dreams, if you live purposefully and remain focused on your ambitions your life will likely be full of joy. That being said, even if you are committed to your success it can be easy to become distracted. For example, while writing this book I often found myself distracted by household chores. This usually occurred when I hit a roadblock. The roadblock sometimes consisted of a struggle to connect paragraphs and at other times I was debating over what quote to use. Whatever the obstacle, my concentration would become unfocused if I saw a pile of dirty laundry or smudges on the coffee table. I allowed the environment to serve as a diversion, would stop writing and attend to the chore. Completing the task resulted in immediate gratification which was an inappropriate resolution to the dissatisfaction I was experiencing while writing. Unfortunately, the sense of accomplishment I obtained by completing the task was fleeting and my frustration returned, often to a larger degree, as I returned to writing and struggled to regain my flow. Perhaps had I not allowed my attention to be diverted, but instead had ridden the tide of creativity I would have saved myself some grief and accomplished my goal of completing this book sooner. You may be like me and find that distractions cause you to lose focus, take you off course and create obstacles that hinder your achievements.

Distractions come in all shapes and sizes and are too numerous to discuss every single one. In this chapter, a focus will be placed on the most common distractions and the simple steps you can take to overcome them. The most ubiquitous distraction you will face is the people in your life. Throughout the book, the various ways individuals influence you have been discussed. As we've discovered, that influence may or may not be supportive of your inner voice. Those who are not supportive of your inner voice can serve as a distraction and lead you away from your goals. For example, the jealous co-worker that offers seemingly helpful advice that causes you to make errors or the parent who belittles his or her child. There are and will be many of these individuals, but fortunately you are not limited to these interactions. Every day you have the opportunity to cultivate relationships with individuals that feed your soul and are supportive of your beliefs and desires. I lovingly call these individuals my "tribe." By nurturing these relationships, you are choosing to live purposefully, and your tribe will assist you in furthering your goals.

How do you know someone is part of your tribe? Your tribe will consist of individuals that are both relatives, through blood or marriage, as well as friends. Some members of your tribe will have been in your life for years, others you may have only just met. Members of your tribe may live within walking distance and others may reside thousands of miles away. You may have tribe members that you interact with on a daily basis, but you may also interact with them sporadically. One thing is certain, the relationship you have with each member of your tribe will be as unique as each of them, but what will be universal is the deep respect and mutual commitment you have to one another.

It's important to note, that you needn't expect members of your tribe to enjoy the same hobbies or even hold the same opinions and beliefs as yourself. In fact, don't expect tribe members to always understand your point of view. If a member of your tribe doesn't agree with your perspective, don't fret. Tribe members will respect your differing opinion and will understand that your belief is important to you. Take Ross. Our perspectives couldn't be further apart. I have liberal tendencies, he tends to be more conservative. I enjoy going out and trying new restaurants, he is happy going to the same diner every time he goes out to eat. I like to travel, he'd rather see the sights our hometown has to offer. We are vastly different, and yet we have amazing spiritual discussions. Despite our differences, my life wouldn't be as full without him in it as he broadens my perspective. You will likely feel the same way about the members of your tribe.

Struggling to identify the members of your tribe? There are a number of factors that point to an individual being significant in your life. First, there is an *instantaneous connection*. You might feel fireworks, have an instantaneous attraction or feel like you've known the individual your entire life. It is likely you have met a person and been surprised how easily you hit it off, having the ability to talk for hours and becoming fast friends. Chances are these individuals are part of your tribe.

Next, meeting tribe members often feels *destined*. These are the people you bump into by chance and/or you discover your paths have crossed a number of times. The universe uses synchronicities to ensure your meeting. This was the case with a set of very good friends. Our daughters brought us together after they had an instantaneous connection on the playground. Due to the undeniable friendship, we arranged playdates and found we had a lot in common. As we became acquainted, we also found that there were a number of opportunities for us to meet along the way: at one point, we were neighbors and had lived across the street from one another; both my husband and our friend are Freemasons; and it turns out, we'd been invited to several of the same events as our friend worked with my friend's husband. If our friendship doesn't seem fated, I don't know what does.

The next sign someone may be part of your tribe is you want to *spend all your time together*. The members of your tribe are often your best buddies. You don't spend time with them because there is no one else around, but rather you feel enriched and joyous while with them. In my mid-twenties, I had a dear friend who was like this. We would spend hours talking over a pot of tea. Conversations would extend late into the night and pick right where they left off the next day. We did everything together.

Additionally, when an individual is a member of your tribe, you often think you will be in *each other's lives forever*. The deep connection not only makes it is hard to believe that anything could come between the two of you, it is also hard to imagine your life without the individual. Unfortunately, sometimes these relationships run their course. If this occurs and an individual is no longer helping you grow, that person will no longer have a significant role in your life. This was the case with my friend mentioned above. A pivotal crossroads in my life coincided with her move out of state. While I was saddened by her departure, I was also hopeful. Within weeks of her leaving, my husband moved to Buffalo to explore our blossoming relationship. When an opening occurs within your tribe, it will often be replenished.

Should you and a member of your tribe part, it will be *hard to let go* of that individual and the relationship will always have a special place in your heart. Why? Because not only are you letting go of a dear friend, you are also releasing a part of yourself. The person you were when you met the member of your tribe no longer exists. Within the individual and the relationship resides a part of you. When they leave that aspect of you goes with them. That can be scary and as a result, many hold on to these individuals. Sometimes an individual will hold on so long that it tarnishes the memory of the relationship.

When a member of your tribe is no longer part of your life, you will *never forget* them, rather they will be the people you think about throughout your lifetime. I feel this way about a handful of my past relationship. There are a few individuals I fondly think of and would love to rekindle the past relationship, but I don't. Why? I recognize that we are not the same individuals we once were and reviving the friendship would not bring the relationship we had back to life. In fact, attempting to rekindle the relationship may lead to heartache. So rather than resurrecting the relationship, I reflect on the times we had with affection and take joy in quietly watching their lives unfold on social media. You may find yourself doing the same with a member of your tribe.

It is important to note, that while these are traits common to tribe members, members of your tribe may have all, many or none of the traits listed above. The only factor necessary for an individual to be part of your tribe is that you believe and want them to be. Take a moment now to consider your life, the people in it and reflect on the individuals you consider to be members of your tribe.

> ## Questions to Consider
>
> *Is there an individual who through his or her words and actions taught you lessons that have guided your life?*
>
> *Who was that person?*
>
> *What lessons did he or she teach you?*
>
> *Do you still have a relationship with that individual?*
>
> *How did that individual influence who you are today?*
>
> *What would your life be like without him or her in it?*

Valuing and nurturing the relationships with members of your tribe is one way to live purposefully and minimize distractions. These individuals will celebrate your triumphs, cheer you on and be the ones who offer a helping hand along the way. When you experience joy and success, they are genuinely happy for you. For example, when my first book was published, my best friend Jen was so overcome with joy and pride for me that it brought her to tears. She didn't personally benefit from my accomplishment, but she knew it was important to me and it had become important to her. Who is your Jen?

Unfortunately, if you are like me, you may not always carve out time for your tribe, but rather find yourself spending time with individuals who are energetic drains. Why would we do this to ourselves? Because individuals who are energetic drains are often hard to say no to. You may feel obligated to spend time with them as they may be family members or friends who have been in your life for a long time or an individual who at one time or another offered substantial assistance. These individuals may even purposefully or unconsciously cause you to feel guilt if you don't spend time with them. We all know a person like this. Consider Ashley. In contrast to my friend Jen who was overcome with excitement for my accomplishment, Ashley expressed disinterest at best and disdain at worst. The week my book was released and as I prepared for the book launch, she was visiting the area. During the entirety of her stay, she never once offered a congratulatory word or inquired about the book. Instead, she spoke ad nauseum about her latest hobbies and expressed frustration while I attended to the many tasks at hand.

The interaction between myself and Ashley brought me sorrow. At first, I attempted to bridge the gap by making time to visit with her and express interest in her hobbies. Doing this drained me and took precious time away from launch preparations. As a result, I decided to create space. Instead of dedicating the time to her, I focused on the numerous tasks that needed to be completed prior to the launch. Since this visit, she and I have spoken only briefly. You can be like me and choose to live purposefully by making the healthy choice of creating space in the relationship, either by limiting your interaction with the individual or cutting him or her out of your life completely. Creating space isn't mean, spiteful or vindictive. For me, not interacting with Ashley wasn't because I don't wish the best for her, I just found our interactions hindered my joy.

Unfortunately, while the decision to create space is usually healthy and results in joy, it not easy. This is especially true if an individual or individuals consciously or unconsciously use emotional manipulation. That was the case when my husband decided to distance himself from Charlene. Charlene is a friend who has been in my husband's life for years. There was a point in time where he and she would talk daily, which might indicate it was a good relationship. It wasn't. Every time the two conversed, she would whine about the unfairness and dreadful aspects of her life. She would then turn her attention to my husband and make belittling comments about his weight and lifestyle choices. These interactions caused him to feel judged, diminished, undervalued and hurt. He would replay their conversations in his head for hours, sometimes days trying to determine how he could be valued by her. He found it hard to focus on other tasks because of the way she made him feel.

After a great deal of soul searching and recognizing the significant negative psychological impact this relationship had on him, my husband chose to limit his interactions with her. Instead of calling her daily, he limited their conversations to a couple times a month, at most. When he does talk to her, he makes sure the conversation is brief and topics of contention are avoided.

Due to the limited interaction, he is happier and more focused. He was surprised to find he doesn't miss her and how much their interactions effected his work and self-confidence. He has achieved peace since limiting their exchanges.

Charlene doesn't make that peace easy. When the two speak, she attempts to make my husband feel guilt by expressing sadness over the distance he has created. At first, he gently explained how their conversations made him feel judged and hurt. Unfortunately, she couldn't or wouldn't understand his viewpoint. Instead, she continued to express her hurt feelings and how she wished they could be close like they used to be. Now, instead of trying to explain himself, he responds he makes her a priority when he can. Charlene accepts this response as it makes her feel validated in that she continues to play a role in his life, but this allows my husband the ability to create the space he knows he needs.

Creating space in this relationship was the healthiest avenue my husband could take. He is happier. He is healthier. He is empowered. This space didn't happen overnight, rather it took soul searching and about a year of practice. Nor was creating this space easy. If you choose to create buffers in your life, here is some advice that will make the transition smoother.

First and foremost, understand that creating space is going to hurt. Just like when an individual loses a significant amount of weight, the process is uncomfortable at best and painful at worst. You are learning new habits that both you and the other party are adjusting to. Many fight changes, especially when they put an individual outside of their comfort zone or those changes are painful. Not only that, even after new behaviors become routine, you may experience grief or heartache. Likening this to the individual that has lost a great deal of weight, he or she may expect to feel wonderful. Instead, he or she may find he or she feel unfulfilled. This occurs because while the physical change, the weight loss, may have occurred, the positive psychological improvement may still be in process and the individual may still lack confidence or feel "heavy." When we make physical changes, we assume it will also remedy an emotional wound. Unfortunately, the emotional wound takes longer to mend than the physical as it can't begin to heal until the physical irritation is removed. When you create space in the relationship, you are likely going to feel a void while emotional healing takes place. During this time, you may remember the positive aspects of the relationship and diminish those parts that made you feel bad. For example, consider a time you ended an unhealthy romantic relationship. After the relationship ended, there may have been times you felt lonely and doubted the decision. The questioning likely resulted from the loneliness more than missing the individual. With time and perhaps a new relationship, that doubt subsides. Same thing may occur when you create space in the relationship.

The second consideration to take into account is that while you desire space, the individual you are creating a buffer with may not. If they do not, they may hold on tight and make you feel guilt for bringing them sadness. If this occurs, it is important to remember that you are not responsible for someone else's joy. The only person's happiness you are responsible for is your own. Charlene wanted my husband to bring her joy and she felt she only obtained "happiness" when she had the opportunity to complain to him. Bringing another joy is a big job and an unrealistic goal. In chapter seventeen, we discussed SMART goals and how the only person you can change is yourself. An individual will not experience delight if he or she does not choose to. That is why, your energy and efforts are better served focusing yourself. Focusing on another is simply a distraction that inhibits your ability to live purposefully.

Let's take a moment now to think about the company you keep and how they affect you. First think about your tribe. After you have considered your tribe, reflect on the remaining individuals in your life.

Questions to Consider

Are these individuals the people you turn to in your times of need and greatest happiness? Why or why not?

Do these individuals turn to you in their times of need and greatest happiness? Why or why not?

Are these individuals supportive of your endeavors? Do they push you forward? How?

> *Do they support your beliefs, even if they don't embrace those beliefs themselves?*
>
> *Do they tease or mock you?*
>
> *Why do you keep these relationships?*
>
> *Do these relationships bring you joy?*
>
> *Do you feel comfortable in your skin when you are with them?*
>
> *How do they make you feel in times of conflict or when you don't see eye to eye?*

As you reflect, be aware there may be times in your life when even you and members of your tribe argue. Tribe members may even cause you pain or distress. No relationship is perfect and having a disagreement isn't a problem. A relationship only becomes problematic when two individuals choose to purposefully cause the other pain or disrespect the other. If individuals choose to work together with respect to resolve any disagreement, then the relationship is healthy. While doing this can be difficult, when it comes to members of your tribe you are often willing to put in the extra work.

Individuals in your life are one distraction, activities you choose to engage in are another. Not every task in your life is going to bring you closer to your goal or life's purpose. Unfortunately, activities that do not further your life purpose take your attention away from those that do. At the beginning of this chapter, I mentioned that incomplete household tasks diverted my attention away from my goal of completing this book. Similarly, you may find yourself sidetracked. This is natural and there are many reasons why it occurs. For one, another task or activity may be more fun than the actions that further your goal. Consider an aspiring medical student. It may be more enjoyable for the student to go out with friends the night before the MCATs, but staying in, studying and getting a good night sleep may be better for the outcome. You may choose the fun option over the wise one, which is your choice, but it is rarely without consequence. In these moments, it is wise to ask yourself, *"Is the potential consequence worth it?"*

Not only might one task be more fun than another, you may downright detest a task that must be completed in order to obtain your goal. For example, consider your local evening news anchor. He or she did not graduate from journalism school and immediately obtain the coveted job behind the news desk. Rather, he or she likely had a series of crummy gigs and covered a number of less than stellar stories over the years. These assignments, while likely less than satisfying at the time, allowed him or her to hone his or her skills and prepared him or her for the job he or she coveted. This hard work paid off, since he or she is now the news anchor. Like the news anchor, as you pursue your goals you may be faced with unappealing jobs and you will be faced with a decision to grin and bear it or walk away. Your decision will demonstrate your commitment to your goal.

Finally, the steps you take to achieve your aspirations do not always yield (apparent) results. For example, consider an individual who has embarked on a weight loss journey. To further this goal, he or she changed his or her diet and adopted an exercise routine. Despite his or her efforts, he or she may not experience immediate weight loss. While the scale may not be moving, that doesn't mean change isn't occurring. His or her body may be experiencing significant transformation such as fat converting into muscle, blood pressure decreasing, or the loss of inches around the waist, but these outcomes may not be apparent because they aren't being measured. This may become frustrating to the individual and his or her commitment may waiver, and as it does, a piece of chocolate cake may become incredibly appealing. You may experience the same thing. You may feel like you are expending a great deal of energy, but not seeing results. In these moments, ponder what other metrics could demonstrate movement.

These are just a few reasons why you may be lured off course. Throughout your journey, one or all of these pitfalls will get in your way. Fortunately, it is often relatively easy to identify which activities serve as a distraction. Why? Because you will find the same type of activity serves as a diversion time and time again. For example, my distraction is cleaning and organizing which could be dusting, organizing clutter, or washing dishes; my husband, on the other hand, gets sucked into YouTube videos; whereas, a friend of mine who is a smoker discovered she takes more smoke breaks when she is struggling with a goal; and, another friend spends hours aimlessly wandering a department store having gone in for a particular item but forgetting what that item is as soon as she enters the store. Just as these activities vary and are unique to myself and my friends, your distractions will be unique to you. The common thread is that the activity will bring you immediate gratification. You may even find yourself disguising the distraction as "work" because this validates the diversion and minimizes feelings of guilt. You may even link the distraction to a physical need or health issue, like the smoker or a friend of mine with a sensitive stomach who spends a great deal of time in the bathroom when he just needs a break. Let's take a moment to identify your go-to distraction.

> ### Questions to Consider
>
> *What activities do I find myself doing a lot?*
>
> *What type of activities do I find myself doing when I'm stressed?*
>
> *What activities do I get sucked into and "lose" hours of time?*
>
> *Do these activities need to be completed or do they serve as a distraction?*
>
> *How can I limit the distraction these activities cause?*

Now that you have identified one or several distractions, it is important to note the behavior is not bad in and of itself. In fact, it's likely an activity you will still participate in. For example, my husband still watches YouTube and I still clean. The important aspect to recognize while engaging in the activity is if you are using the task to avoid another. If it is being used as an escape, that's an opportunity to focus on your goals.

Minimizing activities that don't further your purpose is one action you can take to live purposefully. Filling the space created by removing erroneous tasks with ones that focus on education and personal growth is another way to live purposefully. In a purposeful life, an individual is always growing, evolving and learning. Ideally, you will align this education to further your goal. For example, an individual on a weight loss journey may choose to receive nutrition instruction. To further my goal of normalizing intuition, I continue to educate myself on social media platforms in an effort to reach as many people as possible. The avenue you take should align with your personal preferences. You may choose to join a book club, attend a class, reach out to friends you know hold similar beliefs or even travel someplace new. Whatever it is, I encourage you to do something! Education and personal growth allow you to see beyond your current paradigm and opens you to a world of boundless opportunities.

As you choose to live purposefully and minimize the distractions in your life, you will find you are happier, and your dreams are manifested.

CHAPTER TWENTY-ONE
INTUITION

"Follow your intuition, listening to your dreams, your inner voice to guide you."
Katori Hall

Throughout the book, a number of challenging questions have been posed to prompt extensive soul searching. These questions likely caused you to think a great deal about who you are and what it is that you value. Hopefully you found the soul searching beneficial, but you may have wondered, *what the heck does this have to do with intuition and my inner voice.*

It's been said before, but the answer to that question is quite simple. Soul searching turns the volume of the booming and nagging voice of ego down which creates space for the gentle and nurturing guidance of intuition. The ego is neutralized through the careful and purposeful evaluation of your history as outlined in the first section. Upon completion, you can begin to hear your inner voice. The inner voice is reinforced when you reframe your thoughts, words and actions away from the ego towards alignment with your desires. Visualization, goal setting and creation of action steps then assist you in the attaining your aspirations.

As you've completed these steps, you have likely learned to trust your inner voice. You may have also found that it is an ardent cheerleader that relentlessly pushes you towards your ambitions. Hopefully, you have also become aware of the synchronicities and the "happenstance" occurrences that have been strategically placed in your path. You may consider these occurrences luck. You may realize that it is the universe working in coordination with your efforts. Either way you are likely noticing situations that happen too frequently to be deemed coincidence. These occurrences are your intuition.

What do these occurrences of intuition look like? As mentioned in Chapter Two, intuition manifests itself through strokes of luck, vivid and precognitive dreams, finding oneself in the right place at the right time and an inexplicable inner knowing. The more you notice these occurrences, the stronger your faith and trust in your intuition will become and as a result, any energetic blocks you consciously and unconsciously have placed in your path will crumble. Which means the universe can work with you more easily.

If you are still struggling to recognize your intuition and don't feel like any of the intuitive experiences are happening to you, don't worry they probably are. Here is some advice that will assist you in recognizing your intuition. First, it is important to remember that your intuition is not going to tell you what to do, rather it will simply put opportunities in your path. As these opportunities lead to crossroads, you will be faced with a decision. At that juncture, you could choose to seize the opportunity, or you could choose to let it pass you by. Similarly, you could choose to view an obstacle as a reason to reevaluate your choices or you could stubbornly choose to trudge forward and work through the situation despite the challenges. The choice is always yours.

Next, pay attention to your environment for intuition is simply observing and interacting with your environment. The more observant you are of your surroundings, the more apt you are to see the synchronicities. If you continue to rush through life, you will miss the "coincidences." To become aware of your environment, simply pause. In that pause, activate all your senses. Listen with your ears and your gut, see with your eyes, feel with your heart and touch with your hands. At first don't decipher the information, just take it all in. As you do a picture should emerge, but if it doesn't ask questions. Not sure what I mean? Let's imagine you and a significant other or family member are having miscommunications and you wish for guidance on how to manage the situation. If this is the case, take time to observe his or her behavior. While you do, notice the little things that may be affecting his or her disposition. When I did this with my husband on his cranky days, I would often hear his stomach gurgling from hunger. Noticing that, I'd encourage him to eat something and found that when he did, his mood improved. Now whenever he is short with me, rather than taking it personally and starting an argument, I ask if he's hungry. He usually is and eating puts him in a much better mood. Like with my husband, when you pay attention to your environment you will find solutions to your queries are right before your eyes. These solutions will not only be manifest in ways you can tangibly see, but they may also be one's that you just know. Taking time to pause to allow these intangibles to present themselves are important. For example, consider your dreams. Have you ever woken up and vividly remembered your dream and known it was meaningful, but by the time you've made your morning coffee had forgotten it? If you are like me, this has happened more than once. That dream may have been held nuggets of information and assisted you on your path. If you are prone to vivid dreams and even if you are not, take a moment to journal in the morning. You will be surprised with the outcome.

In addition to taking time to decipher and reflect on your dreams and morning inspirations, take time to just sit in quiet reflection. This could be meditation or simply sitting quietly and allowing your thoughts to flow. Having a sheet of paper handy will be beneficial as you will likely find you are flooded with beneficial thoughts and feelings you did not expect. A piece of paper will allow you to capture the inspiration.

As you take the time to stop and pause you may notice the manifestations of intuition, but you may not trust them. You may question, *"Do I want this so badly that I am making it up?"* In response to this question, I often tell people that if they think a situation or thought is their intuition, it probably is. This is especially true if the occurrences are outside of one's control. For example, an individual hears a song he or she correlates to a deceased loved one at the moment he or she is thinking about that loved one; or, an individual asks the universe to present a sign of positive events on the horizon and then receives designated sign. The song playing and the sign appearing is outside of the individual's control, and yet they appear at the appropriate times. An individual can't plan on the song playing or the sign appearing, it just happens. In these moments, if you continue to question whether your ego is creating the circumstance or it is truly intuition, evaluate the situation and determine if you could have made the event occur. If you could have arranged the situation, it may not have been intuition. Going back to the song playing and you believing it was from a loved one. If you were thinking of the deceased loved one and decided to play a CD that contained the designated song, the song playing is not your intuition, but had you heard the song on the radio or television, it is.

Noticing your intuition isn't always easy and there will be many times that you know a situation is important, but at the time don't know why. Don't try to figure it all out right away, rather hold on to it. The more you do, the more you will find yourself able to interpret the messages coming your way and the more intuitive you will become.

CHAPTER TWENTY-TWO
GO FORTH & CONQUER

"You can do anything you set your mind to."
Benjamin Franklin

You have been provided with the tools to manifest your desires, now is the time to dream big, go forth and achieve them. As you do, I leave you with the following advice. First, understand that attaining the goals you have outlined for yourself in the previous chapters is going to require time, patience and hard work. The actions you take today are simply planting the seeds of the fruit that will blossom in the future. Like planting seeds where some grow and some do not, some of your endeavors to further your ambitions will be prosperous and others will not. For any of the seeds to sprout, however, you must tend to them and ensure the soil is both plentiful in nutrients and water. You must continuously tend to your aspirations and you mustn't become complacent once you begin to witness success. Consider the seedling, it takes time to grow from a sapling to a fruit bearing plant, similarly your goals will take time to mature. You must have patience while the fruit ripens, for if it is plucked too soon it will be sour and unpalatable. If you are like the farmer waiting on his or her harvest, your hard work and patience will pay off with a plentiful bounty.

Dedication to one's aspirations, like tending to a garden, is a lot of hard work. The work and dedication are important, but it is also important to remember that ultimately life is not about the destination, rather it is about the journey and the experiences you have along the way. With that in mind, don't work so hard that you forget to have fun and cherish the moments along the way. How do you do this? Stop rushing. Don't see life as one chore after another. Instead, be present and appreciate today. You may accomplish this by breaking into a midafternoon dance party and shaking your booty like no one is watching; or, you may choose to leisurely sip your morning coffee while snuggled under an afghan; or, rather than trying to fit in as much into a day as possible, you can choose to focus on one activity where you show up early and are the last one to leave; or, simply put the phone away and stop responding to texts and emails, and instead engage in conversation with a friend or family member; whatever the activity you choose to engage in, give it your full attention. Focus on the quality and value of your experiences, not the quantity. Stop trying to multi-task and go all in. By being all in, you allow the experience and joy to flood through every cell of your body.

Focused attention to tasks in all aspects of your life is important, but it is especially applicable to the work geared towards furthering your goals. As mentioned above, your commitment will pay off if you plant and tend to the seeds of your aspirations. Unfortunately, the road to success does not only require extensive work, it's often bumpy. Continuing the gardening metaphor, the farmer may face inclement weather or animals munching on the produce. These are obstacles are outside his or her control and may or may not easily be neutralized. Like the farmer, you WILL have setbacks and when they occur you will have the following choice: you can choose to be dissuaded and give up on your dreams or you can appreciate and embrace the lessons learned and opportunities that have materialized as a result of the obstacle. There is opportunity in every situation, if you choose to find it.

Identifying the opportunity isn't always easy, especially when you encounter lousy situations such as the agriculturist dealing with inclement weather or pests. In the moment of mitigating the damage, the individual may feel distress, but if he or she views the situation from a different angle he or she may find the silver lining. Take the weather on a harvest. A frost may decimate a crop of strawberries, but it causes swiss chard and beets to become sweeter. At first switching one's perspective is challenging. Fortunately, it does become easier with time as you condition yourself to seek out the opportunity. As you do, you will discover that the universe works in mysterious ways to align you towards your desires and life purpose. When you avert your attention from the negative and instead take time to appreciate the synchronicities and magical alignments that occur within your everyday life.

The techniques provided to you throughout this book, will assist you in finding the magic. Not sure what that process is, let me remind you. First, identify where the ego is speaking and why you are being reactive to a situation by reflecting on your history. Once you have awareness of the motivations of your ego, tell it to take a hike, give yourself a pep talk and remind yourself it has no place in a purposeful life. Next remind yourself of your goals and ponder what opportunities exist in your present situation that will further the goals you visualized. And finally, go forth and conquer. The world is yours for the taking. Take it.

APPENDIX

Chapter Two: Genetics

- *Do you have relatives that are mediums, psychics, tea leaf or tarot readers, or something else?*
- *Have your relatives expressed experiences that lead you to believe they have had communication with deceased loved ones either through visions, signs or dreams?*
- *Has your mother, father, siblings or grandparents had an experience in which they have seen a ghost? If they have, was it once or on numerous occasions?*
- *Have experiences like these occurred to numerous people in your family?*
- *Have you had episodes of intuition? How often?*
- *Do your family members have episodes of intuition?*
- *Of your intuitive experiences what occurs most frequently? What about for your relatives?*
- *Does intuition manifest in you or your family another way? If so, how?*
- *When intuition strikes, do you listen? If so, are the outcomes rewarding?*

Chapter Three: Parents & Caregivers

- *How do you believe your caregivers would have responded to paranormal experiences?*
- *Would the response have been positive, negative or nonexistent?*
- *What experiences have you had that lead you to believe your caregivers would respond in a particular manner? Do you have a similar story?*
- *How would they have shared the story? Or would they have kept quiet?*

- *What makes you believe this would have been the way they responded?*
- *Were your parents unnerved by the paranormal?*
- *Did your caregivers discuss death with you?*
- *Did your parents or caregivers believe in intuition and/or the paranormal? Do you know?*
- *Do you recall a situation or occurrence that could be classified as paranormal that took place in your childhood home? How did your parents or caregivers react?*
- *Were there a number of these stories? Or were these stories few and far between?*
- *If stories were recounted, were they told with pride? Or was the story told in hushed tones?*
- *Can you talk to your parents about your intuitive development today? How do they respond?*
- *When you think about the story/stories, how does it make you feel about intuition? Or how does the lack of a story impact you?*
- *Do you think the environment provided by your parents or caregivers helped your intuition?*
- *What goals and aspirations did your parents have for you? Was there a direction they encouraged over another?*
- *Do you feel as though your parents ever lived vicariously through you?*
- *Are your hopes and dreams the same as your parents'? Or, do they differ?*
- *Do you feel your parents' beliefs have influenced your own goals and dreams? If yes, how so?*
- *Have you taken steps to make them happy? If yes, have you sacrificed your own goals?*
- *How have your parents supported the development and execution of your goals?*

Chapter Four: Childhood Peers & Siblings

- *Do you have siblings? If so, how would you describe your relationship with them?*
- *What are your earliest memories of childhood friendships? Did you have friendships before elementary school?*
- *Did you choose your friends? Or were the friendships based upon your parents' friendships?*
- *Did you find it easy to make friends in unfamiliar circumstances? Why or why not?*
- *Did you see these friends frequently? Or were the interactions sporadic?*
- *What feelings do your friendships ignite?*
- *Why did you choose the person you did?*
- *How has this person supported you in the past?*
- *Why has this person supported you in the past? What were his or her motivations?*
- *What did/do you gain from this friendship?*
- *Is this person currently in your life? If not, why? If so, how does he or she support you today?*
- *What did/does he or she gain from the friendship?*
- *How has he or she impacted who you are today?*
- *Was there a time in your childhood when your peers made you feel different or unaccepted?*
- *Was there a time you forced yourself to be brave in front of friends despite being scared?*
- *When you consider the times you were different, are you still different? Or did you adapt your behavior to be in alignment with your friends?*
- *How do these reflections make you feel today? Do you feel closure? Or does discomfort remain?*
- *Do you remember having imaginary friends, seeing spirit or auras, or feeling energy when you were little? If so, when did that stop?*

- *When would you say you "grew up"?*
- *When was your innocence was shattered?*
- *Do you recall a time when you felt as though you had to be brave, even though you were terrified?*
- *Was there a situation that made you realize your beliefs were different from your friends? How did it make you feel? How did you respond?*
- *Was there a time when your friends' actions hurt you to the core? Why did it hurt?*
- *When you and a peer(s) disagree, do you stand up for what you believe in? Or do you remain quiet?*
- *Have you allowed others to define you? Or have you marched to the beat of your own drum?*
- *Do you show your friends your true self? Or do you hide that from them?*
- *Do past experiences with friends impact your present actions?*

Chapter Five: Adult Peers

- *Have you encountered a situation in your personal or professional relationships where you have been demeaned and diminished due to your beliefs?*
- *If so, what tactics did the offender use in his or her attempt to control or change you? Were his or her methods outwardly aggressive or passive?*
- *Did the assaults to you occur from the onset, or did they occur gradually over time?*
- *Which fears did he or she uncover and exploit?*
- *How did you respond to the aggression? Did you ignore it or did you stand up for yourself?*
- *Did the individual's opinion affect the way you view yourself? Have you changed because of it?*
- *How did it make you feel? How do you feel about it today? Did this situation affect future situations?*

- *Is there a time you spent trying to force a relationship, personal or professional? If so, how did it end? How do you feel about it today?*
- *Is there a situation in your life today that you are trying to force? Why?*
- *What in your life would bring you happiness?*
- *What situations support this happiness? What situations hinder it?*

Chapter Six: Institutions

- *What organizations are/have you been affiliated?*
- *What attracted you to these organizations?*
- *How did these organizations impact you? Was it positive or negative?*
- *What are the mission/vision statements of these organizations?*
- *Do these mission/vision statements define who you are? Are they in alignment with your goals?*

Chapter Seven: School

- *In the educational system you were enrolled, was a focus placed on repetitive learning and test scores or were you encouraged to think outside the box?*
- *Did you feel comfortable and supported in school?*
- *Did you feel like you succeeded in school?*
- *When you failed, were you encouraged?*
- *What did your education prepare you for?*
- *What were the greatest lessons you learned from your educational system?*
- *Did you feel nurtured by your teachers?*
- *Did you have a teacher who was supportive of your development positively or negatively? How?*
- *How does that educator resonate with you today? How did he or she impact your inner dialogue?*

Chapter Eight: The Workplace
- *Is there a current or previous boss that made you feel nurtured? What traits did they possess?*
- *How would you categorize the relationships within your work environment? Why?*
- *How does your work environment impact you?*
- *Does a past work environment influence you?*
- *What is the mission statement of the organization?*
- *In what ways was this mission executed within the work place?*
- *What attracted you to the organization?*
- *How does the organization's mission align with your own belief system?*
- *Have you changed since working there? If yes, how?*

Chapter Nine: Religion
- *Were you raised within a religion? If so, what?*
- *What are the religion's primary teachings?*
- *Do you embrace those ideologies and tenets today? Why or why not?*
- *Are you still affiliated with that religion? Why or why not?*
- *If you are not affiliated with that religion, are you affiliated with a different one? If so, what? Why did you choose to change?*
- *Were your parents religious? Did they demonstrate the teachings as a child?*
- *How would you say your religious background helped or hindered who you are today?*

Chapter Ten: The Community
- *Were the views within your community more conservative or liberal?*

- *Were the views within the community radical or extremist? Or did they have more moderate leanings?*
- *Was there a great deal of diversity? Or, did people conform to one dogma?*
- *Were individuals encouraged to blindly accept the principles? Or, were thought provoking conversations encouraged?*
- *Did you travel and experience different cultures? If so, what did you learn from your experiences?*
- *Have you experienced a great deal of variety in your life?*
- *Do you find you enjoy trying new things?*
- *If you do, do you find you enjoy the variety? Or do you prefer to fall back on the familiar?*

Chapter Twelve: Tragedy

- *Of all the traumas you experienced, why did you choose this one?*
- *How did the circumstances conflict with the beliefs you held about yourself and the goals you had for your life?*
- *How did you empower yourself in this situation?*
- *Most importantly, what did you learn?*
- *How does this trauma continue to affect you today?*

Chapter Thirteen: Death

- *Who did you lose? What was their relationship to you?*
- *How did he or she pass? Was it sudden? Or did you know his or her death was coming?*
- *What feelings did you experience? What emotions do you continue to experience?*
- *Why did this death impact and change you?*

- *How did this death impact your spirituality and belief system?*
- *Have you moved through the guilt and grief, or have you found that you continue to carry emotional baggage?*
- *If you have moved through the guilt and grief, what assisted you in this process?*
- *If you have not moved through the guilt and grief, what is holding you back?*
- *How is it that you honor the individual who has passed? How would they feel about your feeling their death?*
- *How did this death effect you for better or worse?*

Chapter Fourteen: The Experiences

- *Is there a book you read that caused you to view the world differently? What was it? How did you change?*
- *Is there a time you sought out guidance from an individual that caused you to look at the world differently? How was it? Why did you reach out to him or her? How did he or she change you?*
- *Are you still learning from this experience?*
- *Why did you choose the example you did? How does this experience impact you today?*
- *Have you encountered a person that, while the relationship didn't last, the memory did?*
- *Have you experienced a situation that, while seemingly insignificant, has changed you?*
- *Why does this situation linger?*
- *How did this encounter change you?*

Chapter Sixteen: What Deux You Want?

- *Is there a type of situation you continue to find yourself in? If yes, what are the common threads?*

- *Have you found yourself attracted to the same type of individual or organization or activity?*
- *What role did you find yourself playing?*
- *Were there themes that popped up?*
- *Do you find that a desire continues to manifest itself throughout your life?*
- *How would you feel if any of the thoughts you've just pondered were removed from your story?*
- *What could you not live without?*
- *What memories are striking?*
- *Why are these memories most striking?*
- *What insights do they provide regarding your life purpose and your desires?*

Chapter Seventeen: Visualize Your Desires

- *Why does accomplishing my goal make me happy?*
- *How has my life changed since I accomplished this goal?*
- *What actions did I take that assisted me in achieving my ambition?*
- *What advice do you have for yourself to assist you in accomplishing these goals?*
- *What elements of the glorious future are takeaways you can focus on as motivations?*

Chapter Nineteen: Deux It

- *What do you hope to gain from listening to your inner voice?*
- *What would a life of purpose look like to you?*
- *What do you feel like you are lacking? What would you like more of?*
- *What values are you unwilling to compromise?*
- *What are you willing to sacrifice?*

Chapter Twenty: Live Purposefully

- *Is there an individual who through his or her words and actions taught you lessons that have guided your life? Who was that person?*
- *What were the lessons they taught you?*
- *Do you still have a relationship with that person?*
- *How did he or she influence who you are today?*
- *What would your life be like without him or her?*
- *Are these individuals who I turn to in times of need and greatest happiness? Why or why not?*
- *Do these individuals turn to you in their times of need and greatest happiness? Why or why not?*
- *Are these individuals supportive of your endeavors? Do they push you forward? How?*
- *Do they support your beliefs, even if they don't embrace those beliefs themselves?*
- *Why do you keep these relationships?*
- *Do you feel comfortable in your skin when you are with them?*
- *How do they make you feel in times of conflict or when you don't see eye to eye?*
- *What activities do I find myself doing a lot?*
- *What type of activities do I find myself doing when I'm stressed?*
- *What activities do I get sucked into and "lose" hours of time?*
- *Do these activities need to be completed or do they serve as a distraction?*
- *How can I limit my distractions?*

ABOUT THE AUTHOR

Dawn Lynn is an internationally acclaimed speaker, medium and author. She has had the ability to communicate with Spirit since birth and in 2007, she turned that ability into a career. She has empowered thousands of individuals, from every corner of the globe, to live a more purpose driven life through connection to the universe. She lives in Amherst, New York, with her husband and daughter. They enjoy cooking together, traveling, and mid-afternoon dance parties.

MORE BY DAWN LYNN

One species. One mind. One world. One energy flows between and within us all. It connects us to one another; our environment; the universe; and, your destiny. This energy feeds your intuition.

ONE demonstrates that intuition is:
- Hard-wired
- A Matter of Basic Physics
- Simply Observation
- Not to be Feared
- All About You

In this inspirational book, Dawn Lynn takes you on an insightful journey to get you in touch with your intuition and demonstrate how simple using it can be.

Connect with Dawn
www.revdawnlynn.com or www.lifeofamedium.com

www.ingramcontent.com/pod-product-compliance
Lightning Source LLC
Chambersburg PA
CBHW030434010526
44118CB00011B/631